Student Book

Jeanne Perrett

Contents

UNIT 1 — What do we do on school days?

| Reading 1 | **Fiction:** Billy the Dragon | Page 8 |
| Reading 2 | **Factual text:** After School | Page 14 |

UNIT 2 — Where do wild animals live?

| Reading 1 | **Fiction:** Max and Mandy's Adventure! | Page 24 |
| Reading 2 | **Factual text:** In the Wild | Page 30 |

UNIT 3 — How does the weather change?

| Reading 1 | **Factual text:** The Water Cycle | Page 40 |
| Reading 2 | **Fiction:** Our Favourite Weather | Page 46 |

UNIT 4 — What can you find in big cities?

| Reading 1 | **Fiction:** Open and Closed | Page 56 |
| Reading 2 | **Factual text:** Where I Live | Page 62 |

UNIT 5 — How do we celebrate?

| Reading 1 | **Fiction:** Surprise! | Page 72 |
| Reading 2 | **Factual text:** Amazing Parties | Page 78 |

UNIT 6 — What jobs can I do?

| Reading 1 | **Fiction:** Sam's Job | Page 88 |
| Reading 2 | **Factual text:** How Can I Be an Astronaut? | Page 94 |

Why do we play sports?

| Reading 1 | **Fiction:** Thank You, Ella! | Page 104 |
| Reading 2 | **Factual text:** Sports Rules | Page 110 |

What makes us feel good?

| Reading 1 | **Factual text:** Lots of Teeth! | Page 120 |
| Reading 2 | **Fiction:** What's That Noise? | Page 126 |

Why are the seasons different?

| Reading 1 | **Fiction:** Larry the Lemur | Page 136 |
| Reading 2 | **Factual text:** North and South | Page 142 |

How are we all different?

| Reading 1 | **Fiction:** Mr. Blake and the Ball | Page 152 |
| Reading 2 | **Factual text:** How to Make a Family Album | Page 158 |

How do we solve problems?

| Reading 1 | **Factual text:** Math Problems! | Page 168 |
| Reading 2 | **Fiction:** Escape The Classroom! | Page 174 |

Why is it good to be outdoors?

| Reading 1 | **Factual text:** Great Outings | Page 184 |
| Reading 2 | **Fiction:** Samira's Sea Glass Collection | Page 190 |

1

What do we do on school days?

Listening
- I can understand short conversations about school.

Reading
- I can understand short stories about everyday activities.

Speaking
- I can say what I do every day.

Writing
- I can write about everyday activities.

1 Circle and say.

How many days do you go to school?

1 2 3 4 5 6 7

How many days do you stay at home?

1 2 3 4 5 6 7

2 Look at the picture and discuss.

1 What are the children doing?
2 Are they in school?
3 What day do you think it is?

3 ▶ 1-1 BBC Watch the video and circle.

1 When do they have English? Circle in red.
2 When do they play computer games? Circle in blue.

Monday   Tuesday
Wednesday   Thursday
Friday   Saturday   Sunday

🇬🇧 British	🇺🇸 American
lesson	class
timetable	schedule
We've got	We have

5

Vocabulary 1

1 Listen and repeat.

math · art · science · P.E.
computer science · music · violin practice · piano practice

2 Listen and number.

3 Listen and say. What classes are the children doing?

4 Which classes are in the pictures? Circle. Which classes do you like?

1 (math) / P.E.

3 P.E. / computer science

5 piano practice / English

2 art / English

4 math / P.E.

6 math / science

5 What does Sarah need in her backpack today? Look at the schedule and match.

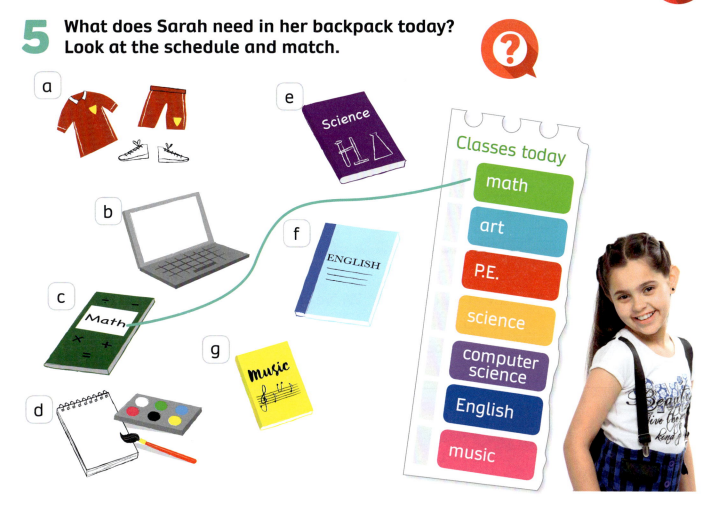

6 What do you need in your backpack for tomorrow? Tell a friend.

Pre-reading 1

1 Look at the pictures. What do you think the story is about? Check (✓).

Reading strategy

Use pictures to guess what a text is about.

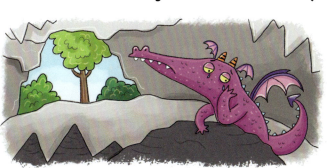

A dragon. He doesn't like school. ☐
A dragon. He wants to go to school. ☐
A dragon. He is at home. ☐

7

Reading 1

2 Read *Billy the Dragon*. Check your answer from Activity 1.

> 📖 **Reading strategy**
> Use pictures to guess what a text is about.

Billy is a dragon. He doesn't go to school. His friends go to school. "What lessons have you got today?" asks Billy.

"We've got **art**, **ICT**, **maths**, **PE**, **science** and **music**," say his friends. "I've got nothing!" thinks Billy.

"Goodbye, Billy! See you later!" say his friends. "Goodbye! Have a nice day!" says Billy. He's sad.

Billy can see his friends at school. They draw in art. They count in maths. They do experiments in science. They run and jump in PE.

Billy is at home. He draws a flower. He counts his toes. He runs and jumps. He does an experiment. Oh, dear! That's not good, Billy!

Billy hasn't got **violin practice** or **piano practice**. He hasn't got a piano or a violin. He plays the drums. Oh, dear! That's not very good, Billy.

His friends come home from school. "Billy! Are you OK?" they ask. "No, I'm not happy," says Billy. "Can I come to school with you tomorrow?" "Yes, of course you can!" they say.

The next day Billy goes to school. He likes being with his friends. He learns lots of new things. He does a very good experiment in science. "Well done, Billy!" says the teacher. "I like school," says Billy!

3 Read and circle **T** (true) or **F** (false).

1 Billy doesn't want to go to school.   T   F
2 Billy's friends go to school.   T   F
3 Billy has a piano.   T   F
4 Billy learns new things at school.   T   F
5 Billy is happy at school.   T   F

4 Talk with a friend. What new things do you learn at school? Do you learn new things after school, too?

Grammar 1

1   Watch Part 1 of the story video. Do Tommy and Suzie like school?

Suzie likes her schedule. Cranky doesn't like art.

2   Watch Part 1 of the story video again. Circle.

1 Suzie **likes** / **doesn't like** art.
2 Cranky **likes** / **doesn't like** Saturday and Sunday.

3 Read the grammar box and number.

Grammar

1 I **don't go** to school.

2 He **plays** the drums.

3 We **run** in P.E.

4 They **don't count** in art.

4 Read *Billy the Dragon* again and circle examples of *doesn't* and action words.

10

5 Look and write. Then check (✓) or cross (✗) and write for you.

	English	2+1 math	art	music
Santiago	✓	✗	✓	✗
Narella	✗	✓	✗	✓
Amy and Josh	✓	✓	✗	✗
Me				

1 Santiago _likes_ English and art. He _doesn't like_ math or music.
2 Narella _____ math and music. She _____ English or art.
3 Amy and Josh _____ English and math. They _____ art or music.
4 I _____ . I _____ .

Speaking

6 Explain to a friend. Read and check (✓) or cross (✗).

go to school by bus ☐   play tennis ☐
play the violin ☐   go to school by car ☐
like math ☐   draw good pictures ☐
walk to school ☐   have English on Thursdays ☐
like science ☐

> **Speaking strategy**
> Keep your hands away from your face when speaking.

I go to school by bus. I don't like science. I have English on Thursdays.

Two checks and one cross!

7 Now tell the class about your friend.

Rosa goes to school by bus. She doesn't like science.

Vocabulary 2

1 Listen and repeat.

tired

bored

worried

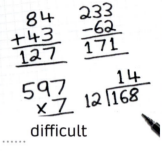
difficult

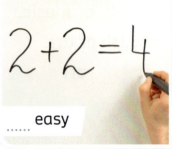
easy

interesting

busy

important

2 Listen and number.

3 Listen and say.

4 Look and match. You can choose more than one.

a
I'm bored.

b
I'm tired.

c
I'm sad.

d
I'm worried.

e
I have an important test tomorrow.

1 Go to bed early.
2 Talk to your teacher.
3 Read your books.
4 Talk to a friend.
5 Paint a picture.
6 Drink some water.

5 **What about you? Choose and circle. You can circle more than one.**

1 Today at school I'm **bored** / **tired** / **happy** / **busy**.
2 My classes today are **interesting** / **easy** / **important** / **difficult**.
3 I think science is **interesting** / **easy** / **difficult** / **important**.
4 When I have nothing to do I'm **sad** / **bored** / **happy** / **worried**.

6 **Play a game in a group.**

Are you tired? Yes, I am.

Are you worried? No, I'm not.

Pre-reading 2

Reading strategy

Use pictures to guess what a text is about.

1 Look at the picture. What do you think the reading is about? Check (✓).

What we do at school. ☐   What we do at home. ☐   What we do after school. ☐

13

Reading 2

2 Read *After School*. Check your answer from Activity 1.

 Reading strategy
Use pictures to guess what a text is about.

After School

What do you do after school?

I go to karate class!

Karate Class

In karate, we kick, punch, and jump. We shout, too. The teacher says "Roar like a lion!" In karate, we learn to be polite. We stand straight and listen when our teacher talks. We listen to our friends, too.

We don't wear shoes and we don't kick people in the leg or face. I'm **tired** after my karate class!

14

3 Read again and check (✓).

	Karate	Gymnastics	Drama
They don't wear shoes.	✓	✓	
They jump.			
They kick and shout.			
They dance and sing.			
They take turns.			

4   Talk with a friend. What do you do after school? Do you see your friends?

Gymnastics

In gymnastics, we run, jump, roll, and stretch. We don't wear shoes.

We put chalk on our hands and feet and then we don't slip.

We're never **bored** in gymnastics. It's very **easy** ... and very **difficult**! I like gymnastics because I see my friends and we're always **busy**.

Drama Class!

In drama, we speak, dance, and sing. We play a lot of games.

It's very **interesting**. We learn about being angry, happy, sad, and **worried**.

We learn how to take turns and listen to our friends – it's **important**!

Grammar 2

1   Watch Part 2 of the story video. Where are Suzie and Tommy?

Do Suzie and Tommy like science?

2 Read the grammar box and write *Do* or *Does*.

Grammar

1	.... you play the piano?	**Yes**, I **do**.
2	.... you and your friends go to gymnastics after school?	**No**, we **don't**.
3	.... your friends like math?	**Yes**, they **do**.
4	.... he go to karate class?	**No**, he **doesn't**.
5	.... she play the piano?	**Yes**, she **does**.

3 Read *After School* again and circle examples of *don't* and *do you?*

4 Write what you do: at school, after school, and at home.

At home

5 Ask and answer with a friend.
Write *Yes, he/she does.* or *No, he/she doesn't.*

My friend's name is ....

Does he/she go to karate classes? ....

Does he/she walk to school? ....

Does he/she like science? ....

> We have karate classes **on** Monday.
> We have English classes **in** the morning.

Listening and Speaking

6 1-10 Listen and circle. Then ask and answer with a friend.

Jenny

MY WEEK

	Morning	Afternoon
Monday	math / English	art / gymnastics
Tuesday	art / science	English / piano practice
Wednesday	computer science / P.E.	gymnastics / drama
Thursday	music / math	computer science / P.E.
Friday	English / piano practice	violin practice / art

Do you have gymnastics on Monday?

No, I don't. On Monday, I have English in the morning. I have karate in the afternoon.

7 1-4 Watch Part 3 of the story video.
Does Cranky like science?

17

Writing

1 **Look at the pictures to illustrate Maria's school day and make predictions.**

1 Does Maria have English at school?
2 Does she do art?
3 Does she play the piano?
4 Does she like school?

2 **Now read Maria's description and check your answers.**

MY school DAY

My name is Maria. In the morning we have English and math. At lunch I play outside with my friends. In the afternoon we have P.E. and art. On Wednesday I have swimming lessons. After school I go to gymnastics on Monday and I have piano practice on Thursday. I like my teachers and my friends at school. I enjoy learning new things!

8 + 1 =

3 **Read the text again. Circle *in the*, *after*, *on*.**

4 **Find or draw pictures of your school day. Then go to the Workbook to do the writing activity.**

✏️ Writing strategy

We use **in the morning**, **after**, and **on** to say when something happens.
On Monday I have piano practice
After school ... .

18

Now I Know

1 💡 What do we do on school days? Read and think. Add your own ideas.

At school we …

make friends   speak English   do math   paint pictures

....

After school we …

play video games   talk to our families   help friends

....

2 Choose a project.

Present your week.

1. Think about what you do at school and after school.
2. Make notes about:
   - what you learn.
   - who you play with.
   - what you like.
3. Present your week to the class.

or

Make a *My Week* calendar

1. Write the days of the week on five pages.
2. Write about:
   - the classes you have.
   - the friends you play with.
   - what you do after school.
3. Draw pictures to decorate your calendar.
4. Show your calendar to the class.

⭐ ⭐ ⭐ **Read and color the stars** ⭐ ⭐ ⭐

 I can understand short conversations about school.

 I can say what I do every day.

 I can understand short stories about everyday activities.

 I can write about everyday activities.

2

Where do wild animals live?

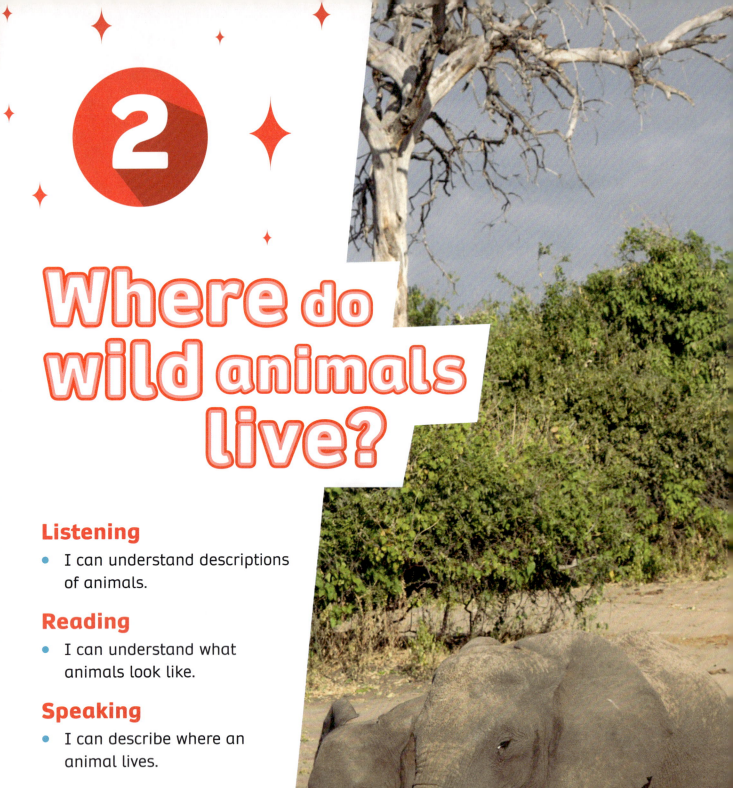

Listening
- I can understand descriptions of animals.

Reading
- I can understand what animals look like.

Speaking
- I can describe where an animal lives.

Writing
- I can write about what an animal looks like.

1 What wild animals do you know? Write one animal for each heading.

Big wild animals ....
Small wild animals ....
Wild animals in your country ....

2 Look at the picture and discuss.

1 Where do you think these animals live? In a zoo? In a hot or a cold country?
2 What do you know about these animals?

3 2-1 BBC Watch the video and match. Where do these animals live?

elephant   bear   tiger   kangaroo

forest   outback   savannah   jungle

21

Vocabulary 1

1 Listen and repeat.

crocodile — kangaroo — panda — snake
cheetah — seal — camel — whale

2 Listen and number.

3 Listen and say. What is it?

4 Which animal is it? Look and say. Then answer the questions.

I think number one is a snake.

No, I think it's a crocodile.

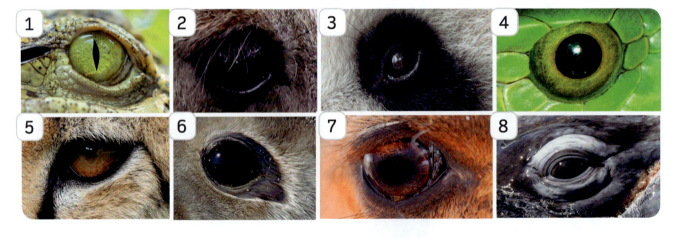

1 Which animals don't have legs?
2 Which animal lives in the outback?
3 Which animal is a big cat?

22

5 Look at these habitats and think of animals from Activity 1 that live in them.

I think the crocodile lives in a river.

Pre-reading 1

1 What do you think he's going to say? Complete.

crocodiles   elephants   whales

Reading strategy

Think about what you already know to help you understand.

"Look at those animals! They're _____."

Reading 1

2 Read *Max and Mandy's Adventure!* Check your answer from Activity 1.

 Reading strategy

Think about what you already know to help you understand.

Max and Mandy's Adventure!

This is Max and Mandy.
"Look at our plane! We're going around the world!" says Mandy.

"Where are we?" asks Max.
"It's the Sahara Desert in Africa! Do you have our camera?" asks Mandy.
"Yes, here you are."
"Thank you."
"Look at those animals! Their legs are long. Their heads are big. They have one big hump," says Mandy. They're _____!

Now they're in the mountains in China.
"I can see an animal!', says Max. Its head is big. Its body is big. It's black and white."
It's a _____!

24

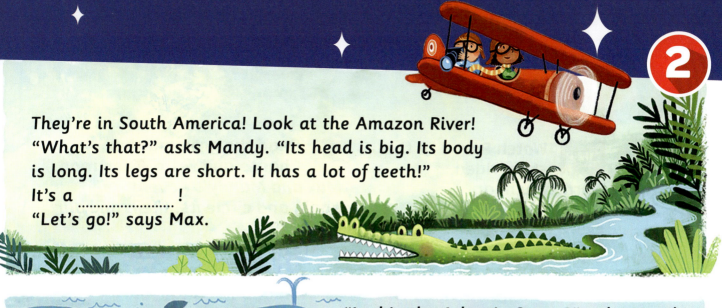

They're in South America! Look at the Amazon River!
"What's that?" asks Mandy. "Its head is big. Its body is long. Its legs are short. It has a lot of teeth!"
It's a ....!
"Let's go!" says Max.

"Is this the Atlantic Ocean?" asks Mandy.
"Yes! Look at those animals. Their bodies are very big," says Max.
"Do they have legs?"
"No!"
They're ....!

Africa again! The savannah!
"I can see a big cat," says Mandy.
"Its head is small. Its tail is long. It's running very fast!"
It's a ....!

"That was a wonderful trip," says Max. "Can I see our pictures, please?"

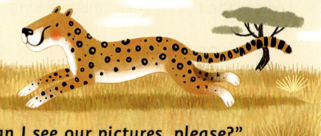

3 Now complete the story. Choose and write.

camels   cheetah   crocodile   panda   whales

4 Talk with a friend. Do you have a camera? Do you take pictures of animals? Where are these animals?

25

Grammar 1

1 Watch Part 1 of the story video. Circle the words you hear.

pandas   crocodiles   seal
cheetahs   tigers   hippos
elephants   kangaroos   whales

Look at the tigers! Their tails are long!

2 Read the grammar box. Choose and write. Then read *Max and Mandy's Adventure!* again and circle *its*, *their*, and *our*.

Grammar

| their | your | our | its |

1 The crocodile has big teeth. _____ teeth are big!
2 The camels have long legs. _____ legs are long.
3 Max and Mandy, is this _____ camera?
4 Yes! This is _____ camera!

3 Look and write. Which animal is it?

1 Their tails are long. _____
2 Their ears are big. _____
3 We are brothers, our mouths are big. _____
4 Its body is long. _____
5 Its eyes are big. _____

4 Read and write *Its*, *Their*, *Your*, or *Our*.

1. Look at the elephants. _____ noses are called trunks.
2. Look at the kangaroos. _____ babies sit in pouches.
3. We are the hippos. _____ ears are small.
4. Hi, you beautiful seal. _____ feet are called flippers.
5. Look at the snake. _____ eyes are yellow.

Listening and Speaking

5 🎧 1-15 Which are their toys? Listen and check (✓).

1  2

3  4

Our names are Sally and Toby. We have a lot of toys!

5  6

6 💬 Look at Activity 5. Circle your favourite toy. Then ask and answer with a friend.

Is your favorite snake green?

No. Our favorite snake is brown.

27

Vocabulary 2

1 **Listen and repeat.**

angry smart fat thin

funny lazy dangerous strong

2 **Listen and number.**

3 **Listen and say.**

4 Read and write. Describe the animals.

1 The hippo eats a lot!
  It's a _fat hippo_ .
2 The snake isn't fat!
  It's a _____ .
3 The camel isn't happy.
  It's an _____ .
4 The panda is always sleeping.
  It's a _____ .
5 The monkey is doing a puzzle.
  It's a _____ .

28

5 What do you think? Check (✓) or cross (✗).

	dangerous	strong	smart
crocodile			
seal			
snake			
elephant			
panda			
whale			

6 Look at Activity 5. Talk with a friend.

Do you think crocodiles are dangerous?

Yes, I do.

Pre-reading 2

1 Read and match. What do you think the story is about?

Reading strategy

Think about what you already know to help you understand.

a

b

1 Its eyes are small. Its nose is long. ☐
2 They're in the sun. They're lazy. ☐

29

Reading 2

2 Read *In the Wild*. Check your answers from Activity 1.

 Reading strategy

Think about what you already know to help you understand.

IN THE WILD

Meerkats live in the desert in Africa. They're brown and gray. They're small and **funny**. They live in big families. Their heads are quite small and their tails are long and **thin**. They make funny noises. They sound a bit like ducks and a bit like dogs! Meerkats eat insects.

Lizards live all over the world in hot countries. They live in Europe, Africa, and South America. They're **lazy** and sit in the sun. They want the vitamins from the sun!

Some lizards can change color. They're sometimes green and sometimes pink or yellow! Lizards eat insects, fruit, and eggs. They have four legs and their tails are long.

30

Hyenas are **strong** and **dangerous** animals. They live in Africa in savannahs, forests, and mountains. They run and chase zebras and cheetahs. They eat big and small animals. They make strange noises. They laugh but they're not funny! They have tails. Their tails aren't very long.

This is an armadillo. It's gray. Its nose is long. Its eyes are small. Its body is hard. It doesn't have fur. Its tail is long.
Armadillos are **smart** and they smell to find their food. They eat insects and eggs. Armadillos live in South America. They don't like cold countries.

3 Write the names of the animals.

4 Read and check (✓).

	meerkats	lizards	hyenas	armadillos
They live in Africa.				
They live in South America.				
They eat insects.				
They eat animals.				
They have long tails.				

5 Talk with a friend. Think of a wild animal that lives in your country. Is it big or small? What does it eat?

31

Grammar 2

1 Watch Part 2 of the story video. Where is Cranky?

An elephant is big. It isn't small.

2 What is it? Read the grammar box and match.

Grammar
1. **How many** legs does it have? **It doesn't have** legs.
2. **How big** is it? **It's** not very big. It's small.
3. **How dangerous** is it? **It's** very dangerous.

a
b
c

3 Read *In the Wild* again and circle examples of *it's* and *it doesn't have*.

4 Choose and write.

How dangerous is it?

| crocodile | lizard | kangaroo |

It's not dangerous. ....
It's dangerous. ....
It's very dangerous. ....

How big is it?

| elephant | mouse | panda |

It's not very big. ....
It's big. ....
It's very big. ....

5 Look and answer.

1 How many legs does the dog have? ....
2 How big is it? ....
3 How dangerous is it? ....

6 Read the grammar box. What do you think? Choose and write.

beautiful	big	dangerous	funny
jump	long	rare	run	small
smart	swim	thin	walk

The meerkats are small **and** funny.

Hyenas run **and** chase zebras.

1 Kangaroos are *big and funny* .
2 Cheetahs _____ .
3 Snakes _____ .
4 Elephants _____ .
5 Crocodiles _____ .
6 Pandas _____ .

Speaking

7 Play a game with your friends.

Speaking strategy

Be open to others by not crossing arms in front of you.

How big is it?

It's big.

Where does it live?

In rivers.

Is it a crocodile?

Yes, it is.

8   Watch Part 3 of the story video. What does the zookeeper do?

2-4

Writing

1 Look at Harry's blog and answer.

1. What are Harry's favorite wild animals?
2. Where do they live?
3. Are they dangerous?
4. What do they do?
5. What color are they?

2 Read Harry's blog and check your answers.

home | about me | gallery

Hi! I'm Harry.

My favorite wild animals are seals. They live in oceans. They're quite big and long. They're funny and smart. They swim quickly but move slowly on land. Seals can be dangerous. They eat fish. Most seals are gray but some are white. Gray seals are bigger than white seals. They live all over the word, from the polar regions to tropical areas. I like seals very much!

3 Read the text again. Circle the describing words.

4 Find or draw a picture of a wild animal. Then go to the Workbook to do the writing activity

Writing strategy

We use describing words to add more interest to our writing.
They are funny and smart.

34

Now I Know

1 Where do wild animals live? Write the names of three wild animals that live in Africa.

....

2 Think. Read and write **T** (true) or **F** (false).

1. All wild animals live in Africa.
2. Some wild animals live in zoos.
3. Some live in rivers and oceans.
4. Some live in savannahs and jungles.
5. Some wild animals live in my country.

3 Choose a project.

Do an animal presentation.
1. Find pictures of an animal you think your friends don't know.
2. Say three important things about the animal.
3. Make a poster.
4. Present your poster to the class.

or

Make animal cards.
1. Cut out six cards.
2. On one side of the card, draw a wild animal.
3. On the other side, write about the animal.
4. Show your animal cards to the class.

★ ★ ★ **Read and color the stars** ★ ★ ★

 I can understand descriptions of animals.

 I can describe where an animal lives.

 I can understand what animals look like.

 I can write about what an animal looks like.

35

How does the weather change?

Listening
- I can understand what others like and don't like.

Reading
- I can understand simple sentences about the weather.

Speaking
- I can say what the weather is like.

Writing
- I can write about what people are wearing.

1 Circle the weather words in blue and the clothes in red.

boots   cloudy   coat   cold
dress   dry   hat   hair
hot   jeans   nose
November   pants   rainy
red   snowy   socks   store
sunny   sweater   T-shirt
today   Tuesday   warm

2 Look at the picture and discuss.

1 What's the boy doing?
2 Does it rain a lot in your country?
3 Do you like rain?

3 3-1 BBC Watch the video. Then check (✓) the correct answer.

What are they making?

ice ☐   rain ☐   ice cream ☐

🇬🇧 British	🇺🇸 American
swimming costume	swimsuit/ bathing suit
sitting room	living room

37

Vocabulary 1

1 Listen and repeat.

windy foggy thunder lightning
storm hail sleet tornado

2 Listen and number.

3 Listen and say.

> There are dark clouds in the sky.

4 Write. Describe the weather in the pictures.

1

2

38

5 Make a weather map. Choose and draw. Then talk to your friends.

Is there a storm in Yellowtown?

No, there's sleet!

Pre-reading 1

1 What do you want to know about rain? Circle.

1 Where does rain come from?
2 What are clouds made of?
3 Does it always rain when it's cloudy?

Reading strategy

What do you want to know about a topic?

39

Reading 1

2 Read *The Water Cycle*. Check your answers from Activity 1.

 Reading strategy

What do you want to know about a topic?

The Water Cycle

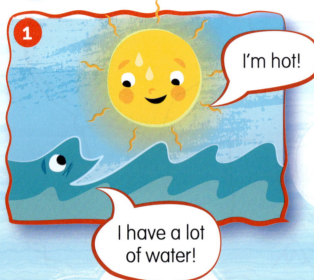

1 I'm hot!

I have a lot of water!

This is the ocean and the sun. There's a lot of water in the ocean. The sun is hot! The sun makes the water hot. Now the ocean is hot, too!

When the water in the ocean is hot it changes. It becomes vapor. It goes up into the air. It goes into the sky.

2 I'm going up!

3 I'm not a rain cloud!

The wind moves the vapor. The vapor changes. It becomes a cloud! Clouds are made of water vapor.
This is a small cloud. It doesn't have much water vapor in it. It isn't heavy. It's light.

40

3 Read *The Water Cycle* again. Label the picture. Choose and write.

ocean   cloud   vapor
sun   rain

4 💬 Talk with a friend. When do you use water? Check (✓). Can you think of more?

4

I'm a rain cloud!

This is a big cloud. It has a lot of water vapor in it. It's heavy. Water falls from the sky in the form of rain, **sleet**, **hail**, or snow.

Now the cloud is very heavy. A **storm** is coming, **thunder** and **lightning** strike! It's **windy**! Look. The water is coming out of the cloud again. It's raining! The rain falls onto the earth. It falls onto the grass and trees. They love rain! The rain falls into the ocean, too!

5

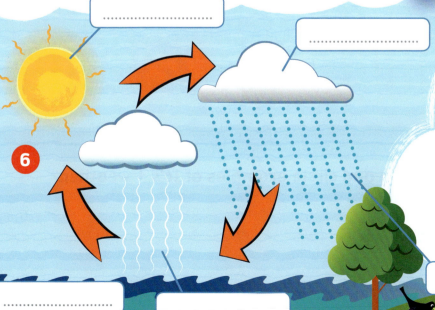

Water goes into the ocean, up into the sky, makes clouds, and comes down again. It goes around and around. This is the water cycle.

41

Grammar 1

1 Watch Part 1 of the story video. Circle the weather words you hear.

cloudy   cold   hot   foggy   storm   sunny   thunder   windy

2 Read the grammar box. What's the weather like? Write.

Grammar

1. It's rainy.
2. ....
3. ....
4. ....
5. ....
6. ....

3 Read *The Water Cycle* again and circle examples of *It's* + weather.

4 Think and answer.

What's the weather like today? ....

42

 Hot. **Too** hot!

 Cold. **Too** cold!

5 Read the grammar box. Choose and write.

cold   hot   too cold   too hot

1 Oh! I can't eat this soup. It's _____.

3 I'm hot today! I like this drink. It's _____.

2 I'm wearing a hat and coat. I can't swim today. It's _____.

4 It's a sunny day. It's _____.

Speaking

6 **Talk with a friend.**

Speaking strategy

Lift your head and look directly at the person you're speaking to.

What's the weather like?

It's really hot. It's too hot today!

43

Vocabulary 2

1 **Listen and repeat.**

- scarf
- cap
- sunglasses
- sweat suit
- sneakers
- flip flops
- robe
- slippers

2 **Listen and number.**

3 **Listen and say.**

4 Look and complete. What's different? Look and say.

He's wearing a .... , ... , a .... , and a ....

He's wearing a .... , ... , and a ....

44

5 💡 **What clothes do you need? Think and complete.**

Pre-reading 2

1 **What do you want to know about what happens when the weather changes? Check (✓).**

1 What clothes do we wear? ☐
2 What things do we do? ☐
3 How do we feel? ☐

Reading strategy
What do you want to know about a topic?

Reading 2

2 Read *Our Favourite Weather*. Check your answers from Activity 1.

> **Reading strategy**
> What do you want to know about a topic?

Our Favourite Weather

The sun, the wind and the clouds are talking.
"I'm great!" says the wind. "Look at me!"
The wind is blowing.
Children are running.
They're putting on their **hats** and **scarves**.
They're flying kites.
"I'm amazing!" says the sun.
"Look at me!"

The sun is shining. The children are too hot. They're taking off their coats and hats. They're wearing **sunglasses**, **flip flops** and **caps**. They're playing at the beach.
"I'm fantastic!" says a big, white snow cloud. "Look at me!"

46

The cloud is snowing. The children are too cold. They're putting on their coats and hats. They're making snowmen. "I'm wonderful!" says a big, black rain cloud. "Look at me!"

The cloud is raining. The children are wet. They're putting on their boots. They're putting up their umbrellas. They're splashing in puddles. Then they go home and put on warm clothes and **slippers** to get warm.

The sun, the wind and the clouds ask the children "What's your favourite weather?" "Do you like the sun, the wind or the clouds?"
"We like the sun," say the children. "We like the wind, too! And we like the clouds.

We like the rain and the **snow**! We do different things when the weather changes. We like you all!"
The sun, the wind and the clouds are all happy!

3 Read and write.

What are the children doing when …

it's windy? ....

it's sunny? ....

it's snowy? ....

it's rainy? ....

4 Talk with a friend. When do you take off your coat? When do you put on your boots?

47

Grammar 2

1 **Watch Part 1 of the story video again. What's Cranky wearing when it's hot?**

2 Look at the grammar box and read.

> **Grammar**
>
> I**'m** runn**ing**.
> You**'re** wear**ing** a robe.
> He**'s** talk**ing**.
>
> We**'re** play**ing** soccer.
> You**'re** wear**ing** caps.
> They**'re** putt**ing** up their umbrellas.

3 Read *Our Favourite Weather* again and circle all the *ing* words.

4 Look and write.

1 The children are _____ in the rain.
2 They're _____ in puddles.
3 They're _____ their umbrellas.
4 They're _____ their boots.
5 The cloud is _____ .

5 💬 **What are you wearing? Ask your friend and write. Then say.**

	Me	My friend
Our clothes		

I'm wearing ... .
You're ... .

 😊 I **love** my scarf.    ☹ I **hate** my sweat suit.

Listening and Speaking

6 🎧 1-28 **Listen to Joe talking about his clothes.**

Draw or .

1. black cap ◯
2. brown flip flops ◯
3. green slippers ◯
4. blue sunglasses ◯

7 💬 **What about you? Talk about your clothes with a friend.**

I love my slippers and robe!

8 ▶ 3-4 BBC **Watch Parts 2 and 3 of the story video. Why is the weather wrong?**

49

Writing

1 Look at Sara's journal and answer.

1 What's Sara wearing?
2 What color are her sneakers?
3 What's the weather like?
4 What does she do when it's windy?

2 Read Sara's journal again and check your answers.

JOURNAL

Today I'm wearing a white and gray sweat suit and gray sneakers. It's windy and it's cold. I like windy weather and I play outside with my friends. When it's really cold, I wear my red coat and my green hat and scarf. I like to be warm. I don't like sleet. It's too cold! I don't play outside then. I stay home and read and draw. I like to wear my silver slippers and blue sweater.

Draw here

Stick your picture here

Sara

3 Read the text again. Circle the color and clothes words.

4  Find or draw pictures of your clothes. Then go to the Workbook to do the writing activity.

Writing strategy

We put **color** words before clothes words.
*I'm wearing a **blue** sweat suit.*

50

Now I Know

1 How does the weather change? Match.

1 It's hot and sunny.   a I don't go out. It's dangerous!
2 There's a tornado.   b I wear a scarf and a coat. It's cold!
3 It's windy.   c I fly my kite!
4 There's sleet and hail.   d I wear a cap and sunglasses. It's hot!

2 Choose a project.

Make a *My Weekend Clothes* chart.

1 Write the days of the weekend.
2 Draw your clothes.
3 Label them. Remember to write the colors, too.
4 Present your chart to the class.

 or

Make a weather postcard.

1 On one side of the card draw or stick a picture of weather.
2 You can draw windy weather, stormy weather, or a tornado. You decide.
3 On the back of the card write about the picture.
4 Show your weather postcard to the class.

★ ★ ★ **Read and color the stars** ★ ★ ★

 I can understand what others like and don't like.

 I can say what the weather is like.

 I can understand simple sentences about the weather.

 I can write about what people are wearing.

What can you find in big cities?

Listening
- I can understand simple conversations about everyday situations.

Reading
- I can understand a written conversation about a town or city.

Speaking
- I can ask where an object is.

Writing
- I can write about where I live.

1 What's your favorite place in the city? Think and write.

The City

2 Look at the picture and discuss.

1. What can you see in the city?
2. Does your city have a big square?

3 4-1 BBC Watch the video and circle. What are they using to make the model?

| boxes | cardboard | paint |
| paper | scissors | tape |

🇬🇧 British	🇺🇸 American
sweet shop	candy store
bookshop	bookstore

53

Vocabulary 1

1 **Listen and repeat.**

bookstore   library   playground   toy store
bank   computer store   movie theater   restaurant

2 **Listen and number.**

3 **Listen and say.**

4 **Where do they want to go? Look and match.**

1 I want to buy a book.   a computer store
2 I want to eat something.   b movie theater
3 I want to get some money.   c playground
4 I want to buy a jigsaw puzzle.   d bookstore
5 I want to play.   e toy store
6 I want to go to the movies.   f bank
7 I want to buy a computer.   g restaurant

5 Plan a city. Talk with a friend and make a list.

In our city, we want …	How many?

6 Think of a name for your city. Then draw your city in your notebook.

Our city is called ....

Pre-reading 1

1 What do you think the story is about? Circle.

> bank   book   candy
> grocery store   library   toy

 Reading strategy

Look for words you know to help you understand.

55

Reading 1

2 Read *Open and Closed*. Then check your answers from Activity 1.

 Reading strategy
Look for words you know to help you understand.

Open and Closed

Tommy is eight years old. He's shopping with his mom and cousin. His cousin's name is Bobby. Bobby is three. He isn't talking, he's shouting! "I want a toy! I want a book! I want some candy!" shouts Bobby.

First, they go to the grocery store.
"It's closed!" says Tommy.
"Oh, no!" says his mom.

"I want a toy! I want a book! I want some candy!" says Bobby. The **toy store** and the **bookstore** are closed.

They go to the candy store.
"It's closed!" says Tommy.
"Oh, no!" says his mom.

"Everywhere is closed!" shouts Bobby.

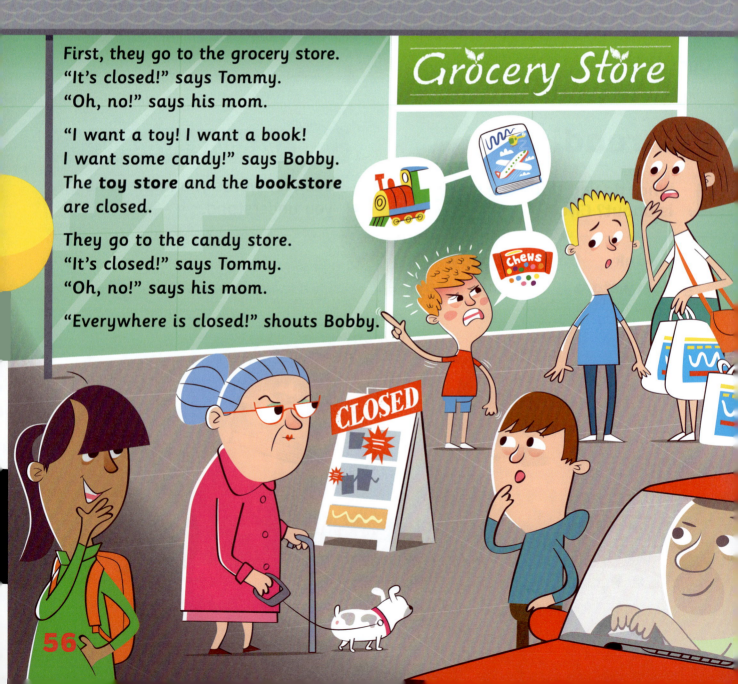

Tommy's mom needs some money.
They go to the **bank**.
"It's closed!" says Tommy.
"And the machine is out of order."
"Oh, no!" says his mom.
'I don't have any money!"

The candy store is closed. Mom just wants Bobby to stop shouting!

Luckily, the library is open.
There are a lot of books in the **library**.
There are toys, too!
"Would you like some candy?" asks the librarian.
"Yes, please. Thank you!" says Bobby.
Bobby isn't shouting now. He's sorry for being rude.
He's reading a book, playing with a car, and thinking about playing on the playground.

3 Write *open* or *closed*.

1 The candy store is ....   3 The bank is ....
2 The grocery store is ....   4 The library is ....

4 💬 Talk with a friend. Where do you get your books from?

Grammar 1

1 Watch Part 1 of the story video. Where are Tommy, Suzie, and Cranky?

Cranky isn't sleeping.

2 Look at the grammar box and read.

> **Grammar**
>
> I'm **not** sleeping!
> You **aren't** sleeping.
> She **is not** sleeping.
> She **isn't** sleeping.

3 Read *Open and Closed* again and circle examples of *isn't + ing*.

4 Look and write.

1 We _____. (✗ clean)
2 He _____. (✗ dig)
3 I _____. (✗ cook)
4 You _____. (✗ eat)
5 They _____. (✗ shop)

5 Choose and write.

cleaning   digging   eating   sleeping

1. The woman is sleeping.
   No, she _____ ,
   she's cleaning.

2. The man is eating.
   No, he _____ ,
   he's digging.

3. The dog is eating.
   No, it _____ ,
   it's sleeping.

4. The mother and son are cleaning.
   No, they _____ ,
   they're eating.

Listening and Speaking

6 🎧 1-33 Play a game. Listen and do.

7 💬 Play with your friends.
Say something and they do it!

You aren't eating.
You're sleeping!

59

Vocabulary 2

1 Listen and repeat.

factory   train station   gas station   street

traffic   small town   fields   market

2 Listen and number.

3 Listen and say.

4 Which place? Look and write.

60

5 What do you think you find in these places? Talk with your friend and write.

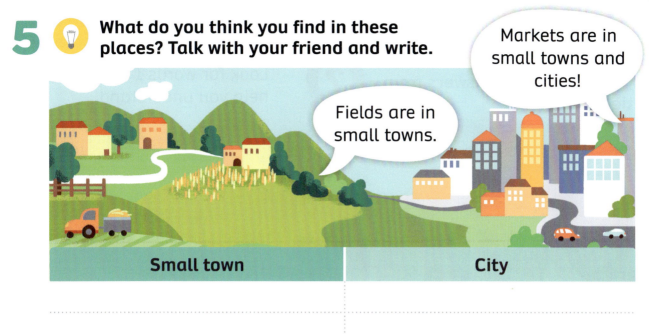

Markets are in small towns and cities!

Fields are in small towns.

Small town	City

Pre-reading 2

1 Think and say.

Reading strategy

Look for words you know to help you understand.

city

small town

A city/small town is.... . It has .... .

big / small   grocery stores / small stores   fields / traffic

2 What do you think the text is about? Check (✓).

a Big stores
b Living in a city and in a small town
c Going to school

61

Reading 2

3 🎧 1-37 Read *Where I Live*. Check your answers from Activities 1 and 2.

Reading strategy

Look for words I know to help you understand.

Scott

Where I Live

Anna

Do you live in a city?

No, I don't live in a city. I live in a **small town**. ☐
Yes, I do. I live in a big city. ☐

Is your school big?

No, it isn't. It's a small school, but I have a lot of friends. ☐
Yes, it's a very big school. ☐

What stores are there in your neighborhood?

There's a mall and a lot of grocery stores. There's a library, too. ☐
There isn't a mall, but there's a grocery store and a **market**.
There's also a candy store across the **street** from our school. ☐

62

Is there a playground close to you?

No, there isn't a playground. There are **fields** behind our school. ☐
Yes, there are a lot of playgrounds. ☐

What do you like about where you live?

I like the movie theaters and the library. ☐
I like that I know everyone in the town! ☐

What don't you like?

I don't like the **traffic**! There's a street in front of our school with a lot of traffic. It's very noisy! ☐
We don't have a movie theater. I don't like that! ☐

Do you have a picture of where you live?

Yes. These are my friends. We're playing in the field! ☐
Yes. These are my friends. We're playing on the school playground! ☐

Are you taking the picture?

Yes, I am! ☐
Yes, I am! ☐

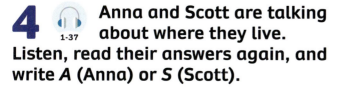

4 Anna and Scott are talking about where they live. Listen, read their answers again, and write *A* (Anna) or *S* (Scott).

5 Talk with your friend. What do you like about where you live? What don't you like?

63

Grammar 2

1   Watch Part 2 of the story video. Where's Cranky?

Cranky is hiding behind the toys.

2 Look at the grammar box and read.

Grammar

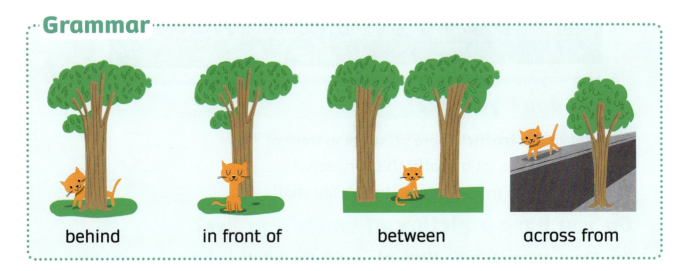

behind   in front of   between   across from

3 Read *Where I live* again and underline examples of the words in the grammar box.

4 Think about your classroom and answer.

1. Who's sitting behind you?
2. Who's sitting in front of you?
3. What can you see between the door and the board?
4. What can you see across from your classroom?

64

5 Choose and write.

> Yes, he **is**.   Yes, they **are**.   No, he **isn't**.   No, they **aren't**.

1 **Are** they play**ing** a game? (✓) ....
2 **Are** they play**ing** tennis? (✗) ....
3 **Is** he hid**ing** behind the tree? (✓) ....
4 **Is** he hid**ing** in front of the tree? (✗) ....

6 Write *Is* or *Are*. Look and circle.

1 .... you taking a selfie?
Yes, I am. / No, I'm not.
2 .... he driving?
Yes, he is. / No, he isn't.
3 .... it sleeping?
Yes, it is. / No, it isn't.
4 .... they smiling?
Yes, they are. / No, they aren't.

Speaking

Speaking strategy

Smile to show interest.

7 Hide an object and play a game with a friend.

One of you hides an object and the other guesses where the object is.

Is your eraser behind your backpack?

Yes, it is!

8  Watch Part 3 of the story video. Why are people angry at Cranky?

65

Writing

1 Look at Micky's report and answer.

1. What's the town called?
2. What's in the town?
3. What's Micky's favorite place?

2 Read Mickey's report and check your answers.

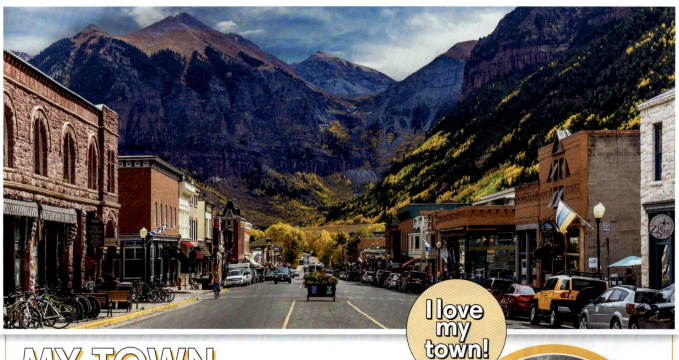

MY TOWN

I love my town!

My town is called Oak Park. It isn't big, but there are a lot of houses, stores, and schools. There is a library and a movie theater. Behind my school there is a playground. My dad is a teacher at my school and my mom works at the bank. My favorite place is the mall. I go there every weekend! There are toy stores, bookstores, and restaurants.

3 Read the text again. Circle *There is* and *There are*.

4 Find or draw pictures of places in your city.
Then go to the Workbook to do the writing activity.

Writing strategy

We can use **There is** or **There are** to write about what's in a city.
There are a lot of houses.
There is a library.

66

Now I Know

1 What can you find in cities? Check (✓) or cross (✗).

1. There are stores and supermarkets. ☐
2. There is fresh air. ☐
3. You can go to the movie theater. ☐
4. People like the traffic. ☐
5. There are banks, libraries, and gas stations. ☐
6. People like playing in fields. ☐

2 Choose a project

Make an ad about your favorite place.

1. Find or draw a picture of your favorite place.
2. Where is it?
3. Why is it great?
4. What can you do there?
5. Show your picture to the class.

or

Make a city or a small town.

1. Make stores and houses from cardboard boxes.
2. Color them and think of names for the stores.
3. Make streets from paper.
4. You can make cardboard people or use small toys.
5. Present your city/town to the class.

★ ★ ★ **Read and color the stars** ★ ★ ★

 I can understand simple conversations about everyday situations.

 I can ask where an object is.

 I can understand a written conversation about a town or city.

 I can write about where I live.

5

How do we celebrate?

Listening
- I can understand conversations about food and drink.

Reading
- I can understand the main points in a short, simple text about birthday celebrations.

Speaking
- I can say what I would like to eat and drink.

Writing
- I can write about my birthday party.

1 **What do you do on your birthday? Check (✓).**

I have a party. ☐
I get gifts. ☐
I eat cake. ☐
I eat salad. ☐
My friends come to my house. ☐
I go to the movies. ☐
I go to a restaurant. ☐

2 **Look at the picture and discuss.**

1 Are the children at home?
2 What are they doing?
3 Do you sometimes go to different places for birthday parties?

3 5-1 BBC **Watch the video and write. How many do they have?**

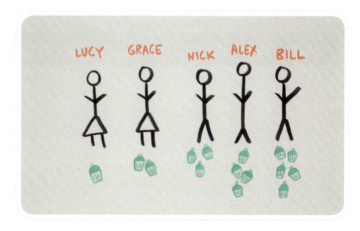

cakes ....
mangoes ....
pieces of watermelon ....
cans of soda ....

69

Vocabulary 1

1 🎧 1-38 Listen and repeat.

...... balloon
...... card
...... candle
...... burger
...... cupcake
...... milkshake
...... popcorn
...... fruit salad

2 🎧 1-39 Listen and number.

3 🎧 1-40 Listen and say.

4 💡 Look at the words in Activity 1 and sort.

You can eat or drink	You can't eat or drink
burger	

5 💬 Which food would you like at your party? Ask and answer with a friend.

- What would you like at your party?
- I would like burgers.

70

6 Plan a party. Think and write.

It's .... 's birthday!
He/She is .... years old.
These friends are coming to the party: ....

....
We need .... candles for the cake.
We want this food: ....

....
We want the balloons to be these colors: ....
We're having the party at: ....

Pre-reading 1

1 Look at the sentences from the reading. What do you think happens in the story? Check (✓).

> **Reading strategy**
> Find the main points of a story.

Lucy has got **burgers**, **milkshakes**, **fruit salad** and **popcorn** for the party. She's got a big cake and eight **candles** to blow out. But Lucy hasn't got friends to celebrate with.

1 Lucy's friends can't come to her birthday party. Lucy is sad. ☐
2 Lucy's friends come to her birthday party. Lucy is happy. ☐

71

Reading 1

2 Read *Surprise!* Check your answers from Activity 1.

> 📖 **Reading strategy**
>
> Find the main points of a story.

Surprise!

It's Lucy's birthday and she's at school. She's talking to her friends. Lucy has got invitations for her friends and asks if they can come to her party.
But her friends can't come. They've got after school clubs and piano lessons.

I've got karate at five o'clock.

We've got drama lesson at five o'clock. Sorry, Lucy!

Lucy is at home. It's four o'clock. Her mum is making cupcakes. Her dad is putting up decorations and **balloons**. Her grandma is preparing a lot of food.

Lucy, can you go and buy some milk, please?

Lucy has got **burgers**, **milkshakes**, **fruit salad** and **popcorn** for the party. She's got a big cake and eight **candles** to blow out. But Lucy hasn't got friends to celebrate with. Her mum needs Lucy to go to the shops.

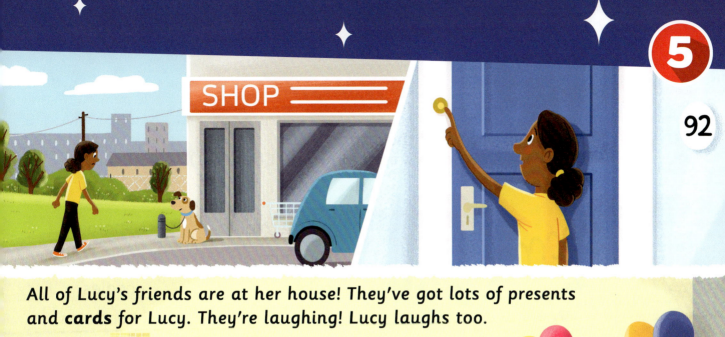

All of Lucy's friends are at her house! They've got lots of presents and **cards** for Lucy. They're laughing! Lucy laughs too.

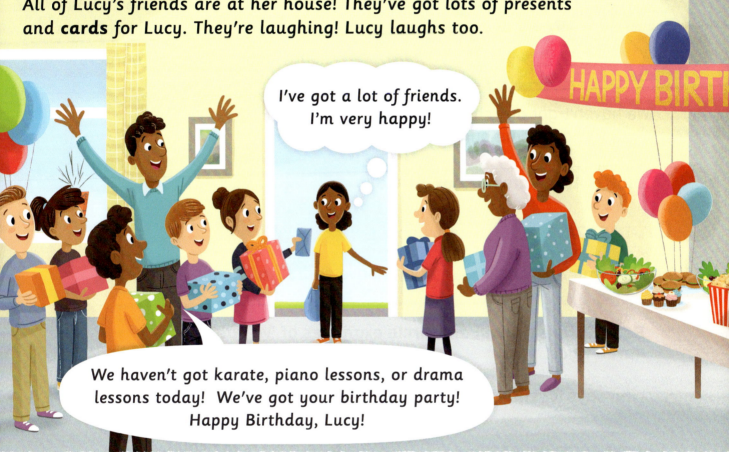

3 Read the story again. Put the sentences in order.

Lucy goes to buy some milk. ☐
Lucy says "Can you come to my party today?" 1
Lucy's friends are at her house. They say "Surprise!" ☐
Lucy's friends say, "Sorry, Lucy. We can't come to your party." ☐
Lucy and her family prepare for the party. ☐

4 Do you like surprises? Do they make you happy?
Do you like surprising your friends?

73

Grammar 1

1 Watch Part 1 of the story video. What's on Suzie's shopping list? Check (✓).

a watermelon ☐	tomatoes ☐
coconuts ☐	milk ☐
cakes ☐	noodles ☐
juice ☐	chocolates ☐
soda ☐	burgers ☐

We haven't got any chocolates.
Oh, I have some burgers.

2 Look at the grammar box. Circle.

Grammar

I have **some** / **any** juice.   I don't have **some** / **any** milk.

3 Read *Surprise* again and circle examples of *'ve got* and *haven't got*.

4 Who says it? Look and read. Write **A** or **B**.

1 I have some balloons.   B
2 I have some juice.   ......
3 I don't have any milkshakes. ......
4 I don't have any burgers.   ......

5 I have some sandwiches.   ......
6 I have some candles.   ......
7 I don't have any popcorn.   ......
8 I have some fruit salad.   ......

74

5 Look and write. Use *some* or *any*.

Shopping list

popcorn ✓   chocolate ✓
beans ✗   cookies ✗
burgers ✓   bread ✗
soda ✓   pasta ✗

I have some popcorn.
I don't have any beans.

Listening and Speaking

6 What does he have? Listen and match.

7 Play the memory game.

I have some bread.

I have some bread.
I have some apples.

I have some bread.
I have some apples.
I don't have any burgers.

75

Vocabulary 2

1 **Listen and repeat.**

ice rink · bowling alley · aquarium · theme park

adventure playground · arts center · swimming pool · nature center

2 **Listen and number.**

3 **Where are they? Listen and say.**

4 **Where should we go? Read and write.**

1 I like castles and pirate ships.   *Let's go to the theme park!*
2 I love painting.
3 I like climbing and running.
4 I like learning about fish.
5 I love swimming.
6 I love bowling.
7 I like learning about trees and animals.
8 I like skating.

76

5 What do you think? Write *Yes* or *No*.

1. You can have birthday parties at home. ....
2. You can climb and run at adventure playgrounds. ....
3. You can learn new things at parties. ....
4. You can play with your friends on your birthday. ....
5. You can go to a bowling alley on your birthday. ....
6. You can have a pool party for your birthday. ....
7. You can eat cake and drink juice at an aquarium. ....
8. You can paint and draw at an arts center. ....

Pre-reading 2

Reading strategy

Find the main points of a text.

1 Look at the sentences from the reading. What do you think the text is about? Check (✓).

You can make pirate hats.
You can wear animal masks.
You and your friends can play in the pool.

Dress-up clothes ☐   **Different parties** ☐   **Summer vacations** ☐

77

Reading 2

2 Read *Amazing Parties*. Check your answer from Activity 1.

> 📖 **Reading strategy**
> Find the main points of a text.

AMAZING Parties

1 ....

Would you like to decorate cupcakes on your birthday?

You and your friends can decorate beautiful cupcakes. You can put flowers, chocolates, frosting, and candies on your cupcakes. Then you can eat the cupcakes! You can have a cupcake party at the **aquarium**, the **bowling alley**, or the **ice rink**!

2 ....

Would you like to be a pirate on your birthday?

You can make pirate hats and flags. You can play on a big pirate ship in an **adventure playground** or a **theme park**. We have paper, glue, scissors, and paints.

78

3 Read the text again. Choose and write the headings.

> Cupcake party   Pirate party   Pool party   Safari party

4 What days do you celebrate in your family? Do you sometimes have parties?

3 ....

Do you like wild animals?

You can have jungle decorations and green balloons in a **nature center** or at an **arts center**, and pretend you're on safari. You can wear animal masks and paint your faces to look like animals.

4 ....

Do you like swimming?

Would you like to have your birthday party at the **swimming pool**? You and your friends can play games in the pool and have a lot of fun! You can't eat your cake in the pool! After swimming you can have some party food with friends. All swimmers receive a medal for attending the party!

Grammar 2

1 ▶ 5-3 **BBC** **What food and drink can you see in the picture? Watch Parts 2 and 3 of the story video and write.**

.... *cake* ....

....

....

....

....

....

....

....

Can I have some cake, please?
Here you go!

2 **Look at the grammar box and read.**

> ### Grammar
>
> **Would** you **like** some juice?   **Yes, please./No, thanks.**
>
> **Can** I **have** some juice, please?   **Here you go!**

3 **Look at the picture in Activity 1. Complete the dialog and write your answers.**

1 *Can* I have *some* sausages, please?   *Here you go!*

2 .... you like .... fruit?   ....

3 .... I have .... popcorn, please?   ....

4 .... you like .... tomatoes?   ....

5 .... you like .... burgers?   ....

4 💬 **Imagine your friend is having dinner at your house. Ask them what they would like.**

Would you like some pasta?

No, thanks. Can I have burgers, please?

80

5 Read *Amazing Parties* again and circle examples of *would you like* and *can*.

6 💬 Write questions about the places. Then ask and answer with a friend.

> **Would** you **like** to go to the movies?
> **Let's** go at four o'clock.

1 Would you like to go to the ice rink?

3 Would you like _____

2 Would you like _____

4 Would you like _____

Speaking

7 💬 Work with a friend. What would you like to do?

💬 **Speaking strategy**
Keep your back straight.

Would you like to go the movies?

Let's go at four o'clock.

Great, see you there!

81

Writing

1 **Look at Danny's description and answer.**

1 Where are Danny and his friends?
2 What are they doing?
3 How old is Danny?
4 What food do they have?

2 **Read Danny's description and check your answers.**

My name is DANNY and it's my birthday today!
I'm having a party with my friends. We're on the adventure playground.

WE'RE PLAYING GAMES.
WE'RE CLIMBING TREES, TOO!

I have a big birthday cake with eight candles. We have a lot of party food. We have burgers, pizzas, and popcorn. We have some strawberry ice cream, too.

I LOVE THIS PARTY!

3 Read the text again. Circle each time you see *too*.

4 Find or draw a picture of you at a party. Then go to the Workbook to do the writing activity.

Writing strategy

too
We use *too* when we add an extra idea. *We're playing games. We're climbing trees, too!*

82

Now I Know

1 How do we celebrate? Think and write **T** (true) or **F** (false).

We eat party food.	......	We read and write.	......
We have balloons.	......	We have parties at home.	......
We do our homework.	......	We make invitations.	......
We play with friends.	......	We sometimes do crafts.	......
We are not with our families.	......	We sometimes go swimming.	......
We sometimes have parties in interesting places.	......	We have candles on a big cake.	......
		We have decorations.	......

2 Choose a project.

Create a birthday party menu.

1. Think about the party food you would like to have.
2. Fold a large piece of card to make a menu.
3. Draw or stick pictures of food.
4. Label the food.
5. Present your menu to the class.

or

Make a party invitation.

1. Choose a place for your party.
2. Think about what to write:
   - your name and age
   - day and time
   - place
3. Decorate your invitation.
4. Show your invitation to your friends.

★ ★ ★ **Read and color the stars** ★ ★ ★

 I can understand conversations about food and drink.

 I can say what I would like to eat and drink.

 I can understand the main points in a short, simple text about birthday celebrations.

 I can write about my birthday party.

83

What jobs can I do?

Listening
- I can understand basic information about jobs.

Reading
- I can understand the main points in a short, simple text about jobs.

Speaking
- I can talk about jobs I know.

Writing
- I can write about what job I want to do.

1 What do you like doing? Check (✓).

reading ☐   running ☐
writing ☐   swimming ☐
singing ☐   talking ☐
painting ☐   listening ☐
cleaning ☐   helping ☐

2 Look at the picture and discuss.

1 What's her job?
2 What's she doing?
3 Where is she?

3 Watch the video and circle. What jobs are they miming?

police officer   cleaner   nurse
mechanic   pilot   teacher

🇬🇧 British	🇺🇸 American
policeman/ policewoman	police officer

85

Vocabulary 1

1 Listen and repeat.

police officer | chef | dentist | vet
astronaut | doctor | hairdresser | photographer

2 Listen and number.

3 Listen and say.

4 Who works with this? Read and write the number.

1 police officer
2 chef
3 dentist
4 vet
5 astronaut
6 doctor
7 hairdresser
8 photographer

5 💡 Think and say. Who works with people?

6 Who does what? Complete the chart.

takes care of teeth   washes hair   takes pictures   keeps us safe
cooks food   takes care of animals   travels in space
takes care of people

Job	What they do
vet	
police officer	
chef	
dentist	
hairdresser	
photographer	
astronaut	
doctor	

Pre-reading 1

1 Sam, from the story, is eight. What job do you think he can do? Check (✓).

 Reading strategy

Use key information to make predictions.

87

Reading 1

2 Read *Sam's Job*. Check your answer from Activity 1.

📖 Reading strategy

Use key information to make predictions.

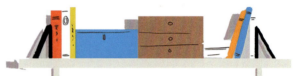

Sam is eight years old. It's his mom's birthday tomorrow.

"I want to buy a gift," thinks Sam. "But I don't have any money. I want to work, but what can I do?" Sam writes a list of jobs "I can't be a **chef** because I'm not good at cooking," thinks Sam. "I can't be an **astronaut** because I don't have a spaceship. I'm eight. I can't be a **doctor**, a **vet**, or a **police officer**. I'm too young. I can't be a **photographer**. I don't have a camera."

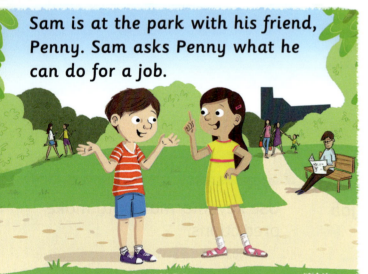

Sam is at the park with his friend, Penny. Sam asks Penny what he can do for a job.

"What do you like doing?" asks Penny. "I like dogs. I like playing at the park," says Sam. "I'm good at running."
"I have a good idea!" says Penny. "You can be a dog walker! You can take dogs for walks at the park."

Sam asks his neighbor, Mr. Clark. "Can I take your dog for a walk at the park? I'm a dog walker. It's my new job."
"That's a good job," says Mr. Clark. "Yes, you can! I can pay you five dollars!"

3 Read the story again. Choose and write.

> birthday gift   dogs   dog walker   running

1 Sam wants to buy a ....
2 Sam wants to be a ....
3 Sam is good at ....
4 Sam takes many .... for walks at the park.

4 Do you do jobs? Do you get pocket money? Do you buy gifts for your family?

Sam works all day. He asks other friends and neighbors. He takes many dogs for walks at the park.

At the end of the day, Sam counts his money. He has 30 dollars!

Sam's mom loves reading. Sam buys three big books with his money. "Happy birthday, Mom!" says Sam. "Thank you, Sam!" says his mom. Sam is really happy he managed to get something for his mom. Mom is very proud and happy Sam gave her a gift.

Grammar 1

1 Watch Part 1 of the story video.
What jobs do they talk about in the video? Circle.

a chef   a hairdresser
a doctor   a soccer player
a pilot   an astronaut

I want to be a teacher!

2 Look at the grammar box and read.

> **Grammar**
>
> I **want** to be a soccer player!   I **don't want** to be a pilot.
> She **wants** to be an astronaut.   She **doesn't want** to be a chef.
> **Do** you **want** to be a vet? **Yes**, I **do**. / **No**, I **don't**.

3 Read *Sam's Job* again and circle examples of *want*.

4 Write *want* or *wants*. Then circle.

1. I _want_ **to take** / **to cook** pictures.
2. They ___ **to cook** / **to go** delicious food.
3. I ___ **to teach** / **to go** to the moon.
4. I ___ **to clean** / **to cook** my bedroom.
5. She ___ **to take** / **to drive** a police car.
6. He ___ **to drive** / **to teach** in a school.

90

5 What do you want to be? Look and write. Choose *I want to be* or *I don't want to be*. Then match.

> 1 astronaut   2 car mechanic
> 3 cleaner   4 dancer   5 police officer

1 ....
2 ....
3 ....
4 ....
5 ....

Speaking

6 Ask and answer with friends. Then tell the class.

Speaking strategy

Think about tips in the earlier units to show interest.

What do you want to be?

I want to be a teacher.

Jenny wants to be a teacher.

91

Vocabulary 2

1 **Listen and repeat.**

check　help　fix　cook

whistle　perform　clean　study

2 **Listen and number.**

3 **Listen and say.**

4 **What do they do? Choose and write.**

> cook　~~check~~　clean　fix
> help　perform　study　whistle

1 Dentists _check_ teeth.
2 Police officers _____ to direct traffic.
3 Mechanics _____ cars.
4 Chefs _____ food.
5 Actors _____ in shows.
6 Students _____ for exams.
7 Doctors _____ people.
8 Cleaners _____ schools.

92

6

5 💡 What do you do? Think, match, and write. ❓

1 I study ....
2 I check *my backpack.*
3 I fix ....
4 I help ....
5 I clean ....

a

b HISTORY

c

e

d

Pre-reading 2

1 This text is about astronauts. What do you think astronauts do? Check (✓).

📖 **Reading strategy**

Use key information to make predictions.

study ☐   clean ☐

cook ☐   check ☐

perform ☐   fix ☐

whistle ☐   help ☐

93

How Can I Be an Astronaut?

Do you like studying?
Astronauts **study** a lot. They like studying. They learn math, physics, English, and more.

Do you like cleaning?
Astronauts **clean** their spaceships. There aren't any cleaners in the Space Station. The astronauts clean!

Do you like cooking?
Astronauts **cook** their food. There aren't any chefs in spaceships. The astronauts cook. It's easy. The food is in packages!

Do you like checking things?
Astronauts can't make mistakes! They **check** all the equipment in the spaceship.

Do you like fixing things?
Astronauts **fix** things. There aren't any mechanics in the Space Station. The astronauts fix the equipment.

Do you like helping people?
When one astronaut has a problem, another astronaut says, "Don't worry. I can **help** you."

6

Reading 2

Reading strategy
Use key information to make predictions.

Do you like floating?
Astronauts float! They don't walk in the Space Station. There isn't any gravity, so they can't walk.

Do you like taking pictures?
Astronauts take pictures. They like taking pictures of Earth and the stars.

Do you like talking to people?
Astronauts talk to each other. They don't have friends or family in the Space Station, but they talk to people on the phone.

Do you like performing?
Astronauts can have fun in spaceships, too. They can play the guitar and **perform** songs. They can sing and whistle, too!

2 Read *How Can I Be an Astronaut?* Check your answers from Activity 1.

3 Read the text again. Write **T** (true) or **F** (false).
1 Astronauts like studying.
2 They make a lot of mistakes.
3 Astronauts fix equipment.
4 Astronauts can walk in the Space Station.
5 Astronauts help each other.
6 They take pictures of cars.

4 What about you? Answer the questions. Say *Yes, I do.* or *No, I don't.*

Count your "Yes" answers.

....

Is being an astronaut a good idea for me? Check (✓).

1-2: No ☐
3-7: Maybe ☐
8-10: Yes ☐

5 Do you think astronauts like their job? Talk with a friend about a job you like.

95

Grammar 2

1 Watch Parts 2 and 3 of the story video. Then read and write *Yes* or *No*.

Cranky likes cooking. ....

He likes studying. ....

2 Read the grammar box. Choose and write.

> don't like   hate
> likes   love

Grammar

I ♥ .... rid**ing** my bike!
He 🙂 .... swimm**ing**.
I ☹ .... perform**ing**!
I 😠 .... clean**ing** my bedroom.

3 Draw 🙂, ☹, ♥, or 😠. Then write sentences for you.

like / love	don't like / hate
I ♥ *playing with friends* .	I 😠 *running to school* .
I ○	I ○ ....
I ○	I ○ ....

96

4 Read and write.

cook   fly

I _____!
I want _____ a chef.

I _____!
I want _____ a pilot.

do   help

I _____ animals.
I want _____ a vet.

I _____ hair.
I want _____ a hairdresser.

dance   fix

I love _____ cars.
I want _____ a car mechanic.

I like _____.
I want _____ a dancer.

Listening and Speaking

5 What does Jody like doing? Listen and check (✓).

6 Ask and answer with a friend.

What do you like doing?   I don't like cooking. I love walking my dog!

97

Writing

1 Look at Jason's pictures and answer.

1. What does Jason love doing?
2. What does he want to be?

2 Read Jason's description and check your answers.

Hi, I'm Jason and I love cars! I love driving toy cars with my friends, cleaning cars, and fixing cars. I love everything about cars! I don't have a car. I'm too young. But I love going to the garage with my dad. I want to be a racing car mechanic. I like watching them work on TV. They check and fix the car very fast.
I think they're amazing!

3 Read the text again. Circle each time you see *like* and *love*.

4 Find or draw a picture of a job you love. Then go to the Workbook to do the writing activity.

Writing strategy

We use **like** and **love** to add importance.
I *like* watching them work on TV.
I *love* going to the garage with my dad.

98

Now I Know

1 What do people do? What can you do? Check (✓).

	checking things	fixing things	talking	studying	helping
teachers					
police officers					
pilots					
mechanics					
me					

2 Choose a project.

Give a job presentation.

1. Think about the job you would like to have.
2. Make notes about:
   - what your job is
   - what you need to do
   - why you would like the job
3. Find pictures of the job.
4. Present your job to the class.

or

Make a job ID card.

1. Find or draw a picture of a job.
2. Stick the picture on a piece of cardboard.
3. Write:
   - your name
   - what you do in your job
   - why you do it
4. Show your ID card to the class.

★ ★ ★ **Read and color the stars** ★ ★ ★

 I can understand basic information about jobs.

 I can talk about jobs I know.

 I can understand the main points in a short, simple text about jobs.

 I can write about what job I want to do.

99

Why do we play sports?

Listening
- I can understand simple conversations about someone's hobbies and interests.

Reading
- I can understand the main points in a short, simple text about sports.

Speaking
- I can talk about my hobbies and interests.

Writing
- I can write about my favorite sport.

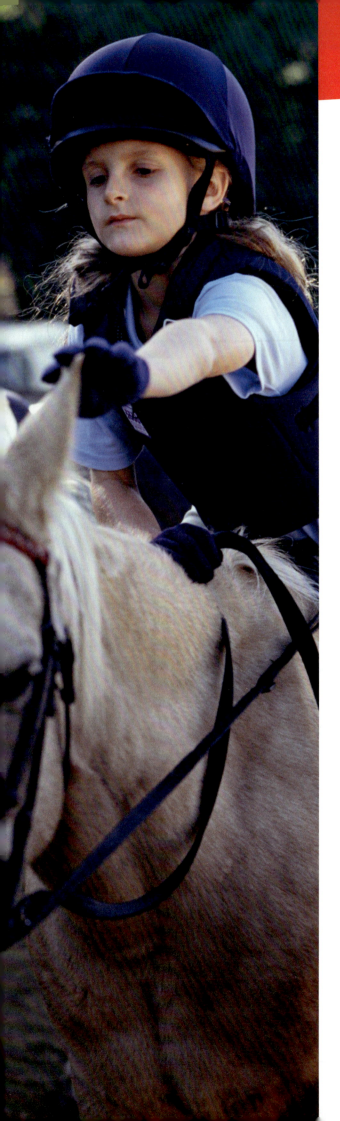

1 What do you do? Circle and say.

I ride my bike and I run.

2 💬 Look at the picture and discuss.

1 Can you ride a horse?
2 What are the children wearing?

3 ▶ 7-1 BBC Watch the video and circle. What sports do they talk about?

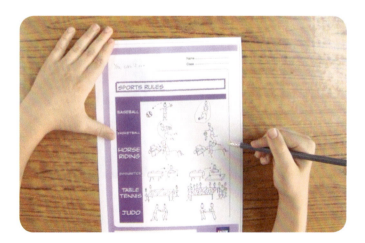

baseball   basketball   gymnastics
horseback riding   judo
ping-pong   swimming   tennis

🇬🇧 British	🇺🇸 American
table tennis	ping-pong
hockey	field hockey

101

Vocabulary 1

1 **Listen and repeat.**

2 **Listen and number.**

3 **Listen and say**

4 Write the sports. Check (✓) the sports you play in water.

.... ☐   .... ☐   .... ☐   .... ☐

.... ☐   .... ☐   .... ☐   .... ☐

102

5 What sports do you play? Write the sports in the chart.

On a team	Only you	With a friend

6 💬 Think of your favorite sport. Talk with your friend.

> My favorite sport is water polo. You play it on a team. You play it in the water.

Pre-reading 1

1 Look at the title. What do you think the text is about? Check (✓) or cross (✗).

Reading strategy
The title helps me understand the text.

Ella helps her friends. ☐   Ella is good at sports. ☐

103

Reading 1

2 Read *Thank You, Ella!* Check your answers from Activity 1.

Reading strategy

The title helps me understand the text.

Thank You, Ella!

It's Sports Day at Ella's school. All her friends are excited. "I'm good at **badminton** and **baseball**!" says Julia.

"I'm good at **field hockey**," says Alexia. "We have a field hockey match today."

Ella isn't excited.

"I'm not good at sports," thinks Ella. "I'm not good at **ping-pong** or **water polo** or **horseback riding**. I'm not good at **skiing** or **paddleboarding**. I'm not good at anything!"

The children are waiting for the race to start. Miss Bright doesn't have her whistle!

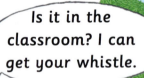

Is it in the classroom? I can get your whistle.

Thank you, Ella!

Ella runs into the school.

She gets Miss Bright's whistle.

Thank you, Ella!

104

Alexia can't find the ball.

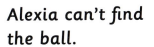

"Where's the field hockey ball?"

"Thank you, Ella!"

The ball is behind a tree. Ella runs and gets the ball.

It's the end of the day. Julia wins the badminton match. She gets a medal. Alexia and her team win the field hockey match. They get a medal.

"This is a gold medal for Ella. She's very good at helping people. She's good at running! Running for whistles and field hockey balls!"

Ella is very surprised! Everyone cheers for Ella "Good job, Ella!" say her friends.

"For me? But I'm not good at sports!"

3 Read the story again and match.

Alexia and her team.   Ella   Julia

4 Talk with a friend. What sports are you good at? How do you play?

105

Grammar 1

1 Watch Parts 1 and 2 of the story video. What sports do they play? Circle and answer.

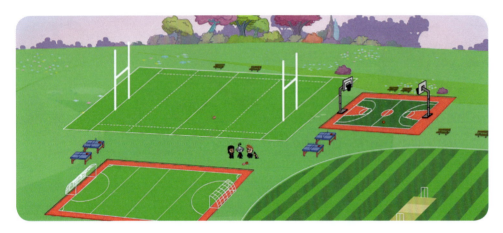

rugby
ping-pong
field hockey
cricket
basketball
baseball

I'm good at field hockey!
I'm not!

2 Read the grammar box and check (✓) or cross (✗) for you.

3 Read *Thank You, Ella!* again and circle examples of *I'm good at/I'm not good at*.

Grammar

I'm **good at** swimming. ☐   My best friend **is good at** ping-pong. ☐
I'm **not good at** skiing! ☐   He/She **isn't good at** dancing. ☐

4 Think, circle, and write.

1 My dad **is / isn't** good at ....
2 My mom **is / isn't** good at ....
3 My grandma **is / isn't** good at ....
4 My grandpa **is / isn't** good at ....
5 My teacher **is / isn't** good at ....
6 My friend **is / isn't** good at ....

5 Write about you. Choose *I'm good at …* or *I'm not good at …* .

1 .... running very fast.
2 .... karate.
3 .... swimming.
4 .... playing on a team.

106

6 Look at the grammar box. Read and check (✓) the correct picture.

7 Choose and write.

> Stop! Run! Jump!
> Don't swim here!

Close your eyes. Count to ten.
Don't look. Run and hide.

1

3

2

4

Listening and Speaking

8 Listen to Henry. What is he good at? Check (✓) or cross (✗).

basketball ☐   soccer ☐   water polo ☐
paddleboarding ☐   skiing ☐

9 What sports are you good at? Talk to your friends.

What sports are you good at?

I'm good at ping-pong!

107

Vocabulary 2

1 Listen and repeat.

bounce   catch   hit   kick

throw   hold   push   pull

2 Listen and number.

3 Listen and say.

4 What can you do? Look and write.

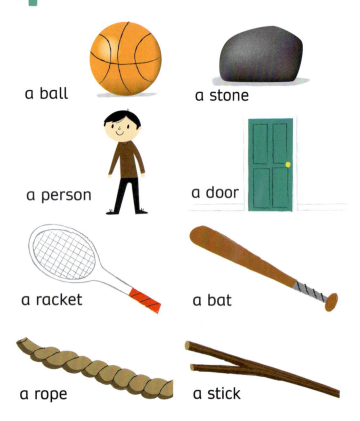

a ball   a stone   a person   a door   a racket   a bat   a rope   a stick

You can …

1 hold *a ball, a bat,*
2 push
3 catch
4 hit
5 kick
6 throw
7 pull
8 bounce

108

5 What are the children doing? Look and complete.

The girl .... the ball.

The children .... the rope.

The boy .... the ball.

6 Think of the things you can do when playing sports. Talk with a friend.

> I can bounce a ball when I play basketball.

> I can hit a ball when I play baseball.

Pre-reading 2

1 Look at the title. What do you think the text is about? Check (✓) or cross (✗).

📖 **Reading strategy**

The title helps me understand the text.

Children's favorite sports ☐

What you can and can't do in different sports ☐

Water sports ☐

109

Reading 2

2 Read *Sports Rules*. Check your answers from Activity 1.

> **Reading strategy**
> The title helps me understand the text.

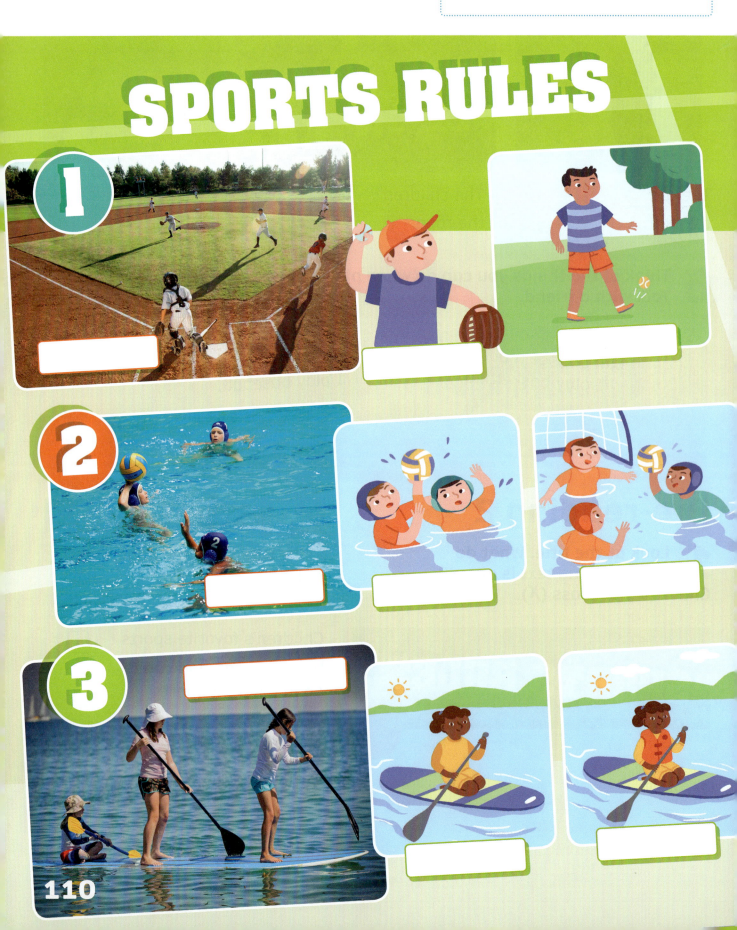

110

3 Write the names of the sports in the orange labels. Then look and write *You can/You can't* in the green labels.

4 💬 Talk with your friend. What are the rules of your favorite sport? What can we learn from playing sports?

IMPORTANT! Please read and follow these rules.

- 🏀 In baseball, you can **hit** the ball, you can **throw** the ball and you can run. You can't **kick** the ball.
- 🏀 When you play water polo, you can swim. You can throw and **catch** the ball. You can't **push** or **pull** or kick and you can't take off your swimming cap.
- 🏀 When you go paddleboarding, you can stand on the board and you can sit on the board. You can't go paddleboarding when there is a storm and you can't take off your life jacket.
- 🏀 In basketball, you can run but you can't run and **hold** the ball. You can run and **bounce** the ball. You can throw and catch the ball.
- 🏀 When you go horse riding, you can sit on the horse. The horse can run, walk and jump. You can't take off your helmet.

Rules are important and make us think about how we behave. Sports help us to work together as a team and to keep trying, even when your team is losing.

111

Grammar 2

1 Watch Part 3 of the story video. Can Cranky play the guitar?

Can you throw a rugby ball?   Yes, you can!

2 Read the grammar box and circle.

> **Grammar**
>
> **Can** I **play** soccer in the classroom?
> **Yes**, you **can**. / **No**, you **can't**.
> You **can** / **can't** hit a ball in soccer.

3 Read *Sports Rules* again and circle examples of *can* and *can't*.

4 Write *Can*, *can*, or *can't*.

1 You _____ run and hold the ball in basketball.
2 You _____ bounce a basketball.
3 You _____ kick the ball in ping-pong.
4 _____ you throw the ball in water polo?
5 You _____ hit the ball in baseball.
6 _____ you take off your helmet in horseback riding?

112

5 Choose and write the rules. Use *can* or *can't*.

1 You can ……… *jump* ……… .   You can't ……… *take off your helmet* ……… .
2 You can ……………………………… .   You can't ……………………………… .
3 You can ……………………………… .   You can't ……………………………… .
4 You can ……………………………… .   You can't ……………………………… .

Speaking

6 Play a game with a friend. Think of a sport. Ask and answer questions.

Speaking strategy

Nod your head to show agreement.

Can you play this sport indoors?

Do you use a ball?

Can you hit the ball?

Is it field hockey?

No, you can't.

Yes, you do.

Yes, you can.

Yes, it is!

113

Writing

1 Look at Dee's picture and answer.

1. What is she good at?
2. What can you do in this sport?
3. What can't you do?

2 Read Dee's school magazine article and check your answers.

My Favorite Sport

I'm good at badminton. You can play badminton with one friend or you can play with three friends. You can't play badminton with a big ball. You play with a shuttlecock and a racket. I like badminton because I like the shuttlecock. A shuttlecock is small and very light. You can run and hit the shuttlecock. You can't kick the shuttlecock. I like badminton because I like playing with my friends. It's good fun.

a shuttlecock

feathers

3 Read the text again. Circle *because*.

4 Find or draw a picture of a sportsperson. Then go to the Workbook to do the writing activity.

> ### ✏️ Writing strategy
>
> **because**
> We can use the word **because** to explain why we like something.
> *I like badminton **because** I like the shuttlecock.*

Now I Know

1 **Why do we play sports? Choose and write about you.**

> on a team   by myself   good fun   good exercise
> boring   a lot of sports   one sport

I like playing sports _____ .   I'm good at _____ .
I think sports are _____ .   I'm not good at _____ .

2 Choose a project.

Do a sports survey.

1. Ask your friends "What sports do you play?"
2. Make a chart.
3. Write the names of your friends.
4. Write or draw the sports they play next to their names.
5. Tell the class what you know.

or

Make a sports poster.

1. Stick pictures of sports you play with a ball on cardboard.
2. Find or draw pictures of different balls.
3. Ask your friends "Which sport uses this ball?"
4. Stick the balls to the correct sport.
5. Show your poster to the class.

★ ★ ★ **Read and color the stars** ★ ★ ★

 I can understand simple conversations about someone's hobbies and interests.

 I can talk about my hobbies and interests.

 I can understand the main points in a short, simple text about sports.

 I can write about my favorite sport.

115

8
What makes us feel good?

Listening
- I can understand how someone is feeling.

Reading
- I can use headings and illustrations to help me understand factual texts.

Speaking
- I can say how someone is feeling.

Writing
- I can write about how I feel.

1 Read and check (✓) or cross (✗) for you.

I'm happy when I …

am in the shower. ☐
clean my room. ☐
eat fruit. ☐
go to bed. ☐
have a P.E. class. ☐
go to the dentist. ☐

2 Look at the picture and discuss.

1 What do you think the boy is looking at?
2 What do you think the boy is thinking about?
3 Do you like being in nature? Why? / Why not?
4 Where is your happy place?

3 8-1 BBC Watch the video and circle. What's the video about?

incisors   canines   molars
drink   food   teeth

117

Vocabulary 1

1 **Listen and repeat.**

toothpaste   toothbrush   mouthwash   rinse

chew   toothache   dirty   braces

2 **Listen and number.**

3 **Listen and say.**

4 Change the word to make correct sentences.

1. You put **braces** on a toothbrush.   *You put toothpaste on a toothbrush.*
2. I'm wearing **toothbrushes**. They make my teeth straight.
3. I **chew** my mouth with water.
4. When I eat meat, I **rinse** it a lot.
5. **Toothache** tastes nice! I rinse my mouth with it.
6. Oh, no. My teeth are **toothpaste**! I want to brush them.
7. My **dirty** is blue. My sister's one is red.
8. Ow! My tooth hurts. I have a **chew**!

118

5 🗨 Work in groups. Ask your friends and complete the chart. Then tell the class.

	Friend 1	Friend 2	Friend 3
Do you wear braces?			
What color is your toothbrush?			
What's your favorite toothpaste?			
Do you like mouthwash?			
Do you brush your teeth in the morning?			
Do you brush your teeth at night?			

6 🗨 What can you do to keep your teeth clean? Talk with a friend.

Pre-reading 1

1 What do you think *molars* are? Read and circle.

> 📖 **Reading strategy**
> Guess the meaning of words you don't know.

animals   candy   teeth

We've got some big teeth. They're at the back of the mouth. They're called molars. We chew with these teeth.

119

Lots of Teeth!

We all like laughing and **smiling**. When we **LAUGH**, we show our **teeth**. Our **TEETH** are important – we should look after them and shouldn't eat too many sweets! We use our toothbrush, toothpaste and **rinse** with **mouthwash** to clean them twice a day. Dirty teeth can give us toothache. But are all teeth the same?

Humans

incisors

Humans have got 32 teeth. We've got some big teeth. They're at the back of the mouth. They're called molars. We **chew** with these teeth. We've got some sharp teeth. They're called incisors. We bite and cut with these teeth. Some people need **braces** to make their teeth straight.

molars

Lions

Lions have got 30 teeth. They eat meat. They don't chew their food. They haven't got molar teeth. They've got four very long teeth. They're sharp. They're called canines. They can **tear** and cut the meat. They've got small teeth, too. The lions hold the meat with these small teeth.

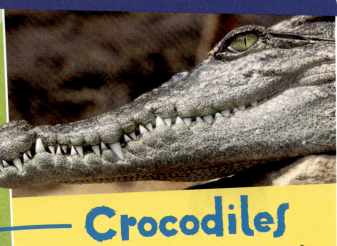

Crocodiles

Crocodiles have got lots of teeth. Some crocodiles have got 100 teeth! When one tooth falls out, another one grows! They grow again, and again, and again! Crocodiles don't chew their food. They've got lots of very sharp teeth! They tear and cut meat with these teeth.

Lots of sharp teeth!

canines

Reading 1

2 2-13 Read *Lots of Teeth!* Check your answers from Activity 1.

📖 Reading strategy

Guess the meaning of words you don't know.

3 Read the text again and write **T** (True) or **F** (False).

1 People have got 22 teeth. ....
2 People eat unhealthy food sometimes. ....
3 Lions have got big and small teeth. ....
4 Lions eat salad. ....
5 Crocodiles have got a lot of teeth. ....
6 Crocodiles chew their food. ....

4 How do you feel when a tooth falls out? What do you do with it?

121

Grammar 1

1   **Watch Part 1 of the story video. Does Cranky brush his teeth before he falls asleep?**

You should wash your hands!
You shouldn't eat with dirty hands.

2 Read the grammar box and circle.

> **Grammar**
>
> You **should** = It's a good idea. / It's not a good idea.
> You **shouldn't** = It's a good idea. / It's not a good idea.

3 Read *Lots of Teeth!* again and circle examples of *should* and *shouldn't*.

4 Write *You should* or *You shouldn't*.

1 *You shouldn't* eat lots of candy.
2 _____ brush your teeth every day.
3 _____ use a dirty toothbrush.
4 _____ use a clean toothbrush.
5 _____ go to the dentist.
6 _____ chew your food well.

122

5 Read and write. Are these things clean or dirty? Neat or messy? Healthy or unhealthy?

clean	dirty	healthy	messy	neat	unhealthy

leave crayons on the desk		wear the same socks every day	
wash your hands		wipe your nose with your hand	
eat lots of cupcakes		put your crayons in a pencil case	
take a shower		put your books on the floor	
do lots of exercise		eat fruit and salad	
put your books in your backpack		drink lots of soda	

Speaking

6 Think about these places. Talk with your friends about what you should and shouldn't do.

> 💬 **Speaking strategy**
> Look at the speaker to show interest.

At school   At the dentist   At the park

At school.

You should listen to the teacher.

You shouldn't run in the classroom.

Vocabulary 2

1 **Listen and repeat.**

hear | smell | taste | touch
hurt | feel | relax | breathe

2 **Listen and number.**

3 **Listen and say.**

4 **Look at the words in Activity 1 and label.**

1 taste

5 **Look at Activity 1 and complete.**

1 I ……feel…… with all my body.
2 I ………………… with my tongue.
3 I ………………… with my fingers.
4 I ………………… with my ears.
5 I ………………… in air with my nose and my mouth.
6 When I sleep, I ………………… my body.

6 What can you do? Check (✓) or cross (✗). Then say.

I can hear the ocean.
I can smell the ocean.

	hear	smell	see	touch	taste	feel
the ocean						
an ice cream						
music						
an elephant						
a toothache						
happy						

7 What makes you feel good? Talk with a friend.

I feel good when I'm by the ocean.

Pre-reading 2

📖 **Reading strategy**

Guess the meaning of words you don't know.

1 Read and guess the answer. Check (✓).

"I can hear **footsteps**," says Leo. "Someone is coming to the tent!"

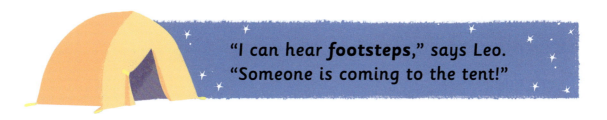

I think the footsteps are the sound of … .

eating ☐   walking ☐   swimming ☐

125

Reading 2

2 Read *What's That Noise?* Check your answer from Activity 1.

> 📖 **Reading strategy**
>
> Guess the meaning of words you don't know.

WHAT'S THAT NOISE?

Clara and her little brother, Leo, are camping. They're in a tent. It's dark.

"I can **hear** a noise," says Leo. "What is it?"

"It's an owl," says Clara. "Don't worry. Owls are friendly birds."

"I can hear another noise," says Leo. "What is it? Is it a bear?"

"No!" says Clara. "It isn't a bear. It's a fox."

"I can **smell** something," says Leo. "It smells nice."

I think it's cheeseburgers.

Cheeseburgers are my favorite food.

"I **feel** cold," says Leo. Clara gets a blanket for Leo. "**Breathe** deeply," says Clara.

*My tooth **hurts**. I have a toothache.*

Clara gets some water for Leo. "Go to sleep, Leo," she says. "**Relax** and go to sleep."

126

3 Read and circle.

1. Leo and Clara can hear **an owl** / **a cat** and **a bear** / **footsteps**.
2. Leo's **leg** / **tooth** hurts.
3. Leo is **cold** / **hot**.
4. Leo can't **relax** / **breathe**.
5. Leo and Clara can smell **cheeseburgers** / **a cat**.

4 Think about the story. Discuss with a friend.

1. What noises can you hear at night?
2. How do they make you feel?

127

Grammar 2

1   Watch Part 1 of the story video again. Then choose and write.

> lemon   smells   taste   tastes

1 These candies _____ great.
2 This is _____ .
3 This _____ of ice cream.
4 What's that smell? It _____ good.

2 Look at the grammar box and read.

3 Read *What's That Noise?* again and circle the examples of *smells nice* and *tastes good*.

Grammar

Dad is baking. The bread **smells nice**!
My dinner **smells bad**!
The ice cream **tastes good**!
The ice cream **tastes bad**!

4 What do you think? Choose and write.

> smell bad   smell nice   tastes bad   tastes good

1 My sandwich is too dry. It _____ .
2 The cake _____ .
3 The flowers _____ .
4 The rotten vegetables _____ .

128

5 **Rewrite the sentences in the text.**

I swim and I feel good.
I feel good **when** I swim.

I see my friends in the park and I feel good.
1 I feel good when I see my friends.

We laugh and we feel good.
2 _____

We play tennis and we feel good.
3 _____

I go to the beach and I feel good.
4 _____

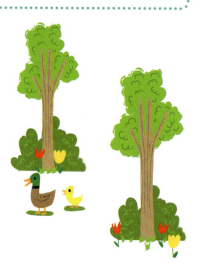

Listening and Speaking

6 **Look, choose, and write. Then listen to Lucas and circle.**
2-18

Lucas

| play soccer | drink soda |
| eat pasta | drink milk |

1 I feel **happy** / **great** when I _____.
2 I feel **tired** / **great** when I _____.
3 I feel **good** / **bad** when I _____.
4 I feel **tired** / **happy** when I _____.

7 **How do you feel? Talk with your friends.**

I feel happy when I have pasta for dinner. It tastes really good!

I feel healthy when I eat fruit.

8   **Watch Parts 2 and 3 of the story video. Why does Cranky go to the dentist?**

129

Writing

1 What makes Alice feel good? Look at the picture and circle.

apples   laughing   P.E.   pears   swimming   teddy bear   tennis

2 Read Alice's poem and check your answers.

I Feel Good When I...

I feel good when I hug my bear.
I feel good when I eat a pear.
I feel good when I do P.E.
I feel good when I swim in the sea.
I feel good when I take a bath.
I feel good when I sing and laugh.
I feel good when I run and play.
I feel good every day!

3 Read the text again. Circle the words that rhyme.

4 Find or draw a picture of things you like. Then go to the Workbook to do the writing activity.

Writing strategy

We can write poems with words that **rhyme**:

bear — pear   bath — laugh

We can write poems with words that don't rhyme, too.

130

Now I Know

1 What makes us feel good?
Circle for you and add your own ideas.

I feel good when I'm …

clean   dirty   at school   with my friends

....

I feel good when I have …

a toothache   good food   a lot of of homework

....

2 Choose a project.

Write an information leaflet.
1. Choose an animal.
2. Find a picture of its teeth.
3. Are they big or small?
4. What does the animal eat?
5. Present your leaflet to the class.

or

Make a tooth poster.
1. Draw and label a big tooth.
2. Find or draw pictures of:
   - What's good for your teeth.
   - What's bad for your teeth.
3. Show your poster to the class.

★ ★ ★ **Read and color the stars** ★ ★ ★

 I can understand how someone is feeling.

 I can say how someone is feeling.

 I can use headings and illustrations to help me understand factual texts.

 I can write about how I feel.

131

9

How are the seasons different?

Listening
- I can understand basic information about times of the year.

Reading
- I can follow the sequence of events in a short text about the seasons.

Speaking
- I can describe what the weather is like in my country.

Writing
- I can write about the weather.

1 **What's the weather like today? Circle.**

1 The sky is **blue** / **gray**.
2 There are **a lot of** / **not many** / **no** clouds in the sky.
3 The trees **have** / **don't have** leaves.
4 The leaves on the trees are **green** / **yellow** / **red**.

2 **Look at the picture and discuss.**

1 What color are the leaves?
2 When does your school year start?
3 Is it hot or cold when you start the school year?

3 9-1 **Watch the video and circle.**

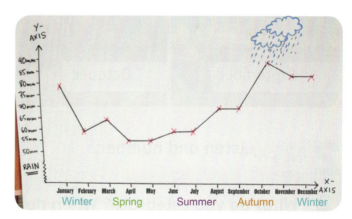

1 What are they drawing?

   a graph   **a picture**

2 Which month has the most rain?

   January   **October**

🇬🇧 British	🇺🇸 American
autumn	fall

133

Vocabulary 1

1 **Listen and repeat.**

January   February   March   April
May   June   July   August
September   October   November   December

2 **Listen and number.**

3 **Listen and say.**

4 What do you celebrate? When do you celebrate? Write.

New Year: January
My birthday:
My mom's birthday:
Mother's Day:

134

5 💬 Ask and answer with a friend. Complete the chart.

	You	Your friend
What's your favorite month?		
What month is your birthday?		
When is your favorite celebration?		

Pre-reading 1

1 Look at the sentence. Which picture do you think of? Check (✓).

> 📖 **Reading strategy**
>
> Visualize the story.

It's December and the sun is shining.

135

Reading 1

2 Read *Larry the Lemur*. Check your answer from Activity 1.

Reading strategy

Visualize the story.

LARRY THE LEMUR

Larry the Lemur lives in a tree in a big forest. It's **December** and the sun is shining.

"What a beautiful day," says Larry. He sits in a tree and watches his friends play.

"Hi, Larry! Are you OK?" asks his friend. His friend is a frog. His name is Tomato!

"Yes, I'm fine now but **June, July, August, September, October,** and **November** are very cold months for me," says Larry the Lemur. "I can't find food when it's cold … so I go to bed."

"Wow. You sleep for months!" says Tomato the frog.

In **December, January, February, March, April,** and **May** it's hot. Larry the Lemur sits in the sun. He talks to his friends and he collects fruit, flowers, and insects, too. He eats … and eats … and eats! His tail gets VERY big.

"Wow. You eat a lot!" says Tomato.

"Yes, but it's OK. I'm hungry now and the food makes my tail fat!"

Larry eats, and eats, and eats.

In **June**, the weather is cloudy. "The flowers and fruits are changing," says Larry. "It isn't hot now."

136

In June, the sky is gray.

"It's raining!" says Larry. "I'm tired. My tail is fat and can help me sleep!" Larry sleeps for months.

It's **December** and it's sunny again. Larry gets up and sits in a tree.

"Hi!" says Tomato. "Your tail is different. It's thin." "Hi, Tomato! Yes, my tail is thin again. My tail grows and helps me sleep in June, July, August, September, October, and November."

3 Read the story again. Write the months.
1 It's sunny. ....
2 It's hot. ....
3 It's cloudy. ....
4 The sky is gray. ....

4 Can you think of other animals that sleep for months?

Grammar 1

1 Watch Part 1 of the story video. What are the four seasons?

2 Look at the grammar box and read.

I sometimes play in the snow in January.

3 Read and complete.

1. I _never_ go to school in August. ☆☆☆☆
2. They _____ go to school in September. ★★★★
3. She _____ plays outside in May. ★★★☆
4. We _____ play indoors in January. ★★☆☆

4 When do you do these things? Write.

> stay indoors   go to the beach   swim in the ocean
> ride my bike   read a lot of books   have picnics
> watch TV   eat ice cream   eat soup

Always	Often	Sometimes	Never

138

5 Look at Activity 4. Then write sentences for you with *always*, *often*, *sometimes*, and *never*.

1 I sometimes go to the beach.
2 ....
3 ....
4 ....

Listening and Speaking

6 🎧 2-23 Listen and check (✓) the correct months.

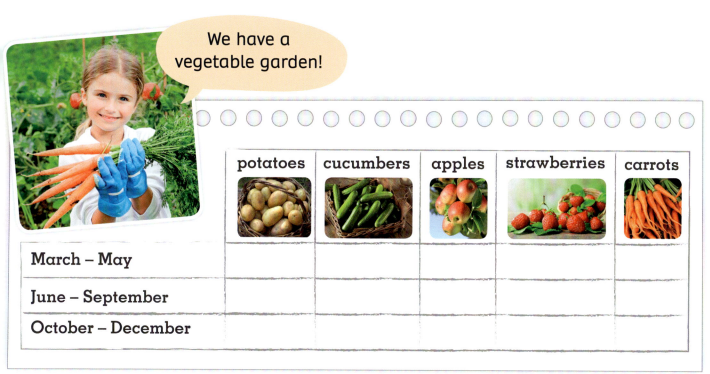

7 💬 What do you like to eat? Talk with a friend.

I often eat carrots. What about you?

I sometimes eat carrots. I always eat potatoes.

139

Vocabulary 2

1 **Listen and repeat.**

spring　summer　fall　winter
seasons　world　North　South

2 **Listen and number.**

3 **Listen and say.**

4 Complete the seasons.

pick flowers
go to the beach
play in the leaves
go skiing

140

5 What do you do in the different seasons in your country? Write.

    eat hot soup   eat strawberries   make a snowman
pick flowers   play in the leaves   start school   swim in the ocean
                wear a coat   wear shorts

Spring	Summer	Fall	Winter

Pre-reading 2

1 Look at the sentences from the reading. Draw and color.

 Reading strategy

Visualize the text.

When it's winter in the North, it's summer in the South.

141

Reading 2

2 Read *North* and *South*. Check your answer from Activity 1.

📖 **Reading strategy**

Visualize the text.

North and South

1

Look at the picture of the **world**. Can you see a line in the middle of the world? It's called the equator. This is a line we draw on maps. There isn't really a line in the middle of the world.

2

North of the equator is one half of the world. This is called the Northern Hemisphere. **South** of the equator is the other half of the world. This is called the Southern Hemisphere.

3

The Northern and the Southern Hemispheres have different **seasons**! When it's **winter** in the North, it's **summer** in the South.

When it's **spring** in the North, it's **fall** in the South.

4 When the weather is hot in the North, children swim in the ocean and eat summer fruits, but in the South, the weather is cold and children sometimes play in the snow and eat soup.

5 In the North, when it's fall and the leaves on the trees are orange, they're green in the South because it's spring.

The Northern and the Southern Hemispheres have the same months. When it's January in the North, it's January in the South.

6 In the North, December, January, and February are in the winter, but in the South those months are in the summer.

In the North, June, July, and August are in the summer. In the South, those months are in the winter.

3 Say the months for each season in the Northern and Southern Hemispheres.

4 💬 Is your country in the Northern or the Southern Hemisphere? What month and season is it now?

Grammar 2

1 Watch Part 2 of the story video. Does Cranky like cold weather?

2 Look at the grammar box. Circle for your country.

How often does it snow in England?

Grammar

How often does it rain?
It **always** / **often** / **sometimes** / **never** rains.

How often does it snow?
It **always** / **often** / **sometimes** / **never** snows.

3 How often does it rain or snow? Look and write.

	Spring	Summer	Fall	Winter
🌧️	✓✓✓	✓✓	✓✓✓	✓✓✓✓
🌨️	✓✓	✗	✓✓	✓✓✓

1 _____ rain in the spring?
It _____ rains in spring.

2 How _____ snow in spring?
It _____ snows in spring.

3 _____ rain in summer?
It _____ rains in summer.

4 How _____ snow in fall?
It _____ in fall.

5 How _____ rain in winter?
It _____ in winter.

144

4 Look and write T (true) or F (false).

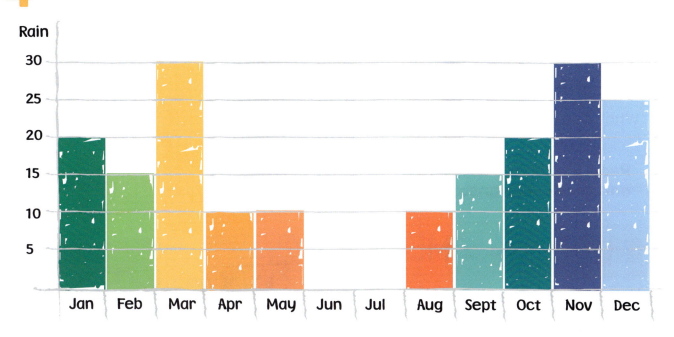

1 It always rains in November. ......
2 It always rains in June. ......
3 It sometimes rains in April. ......
4 It sometimes rains in August. ......
5 It never rains in December. ......
6 It sometimes rains in March. ......

5 Write about these months.

January: *It often rains in January.*   July: _____
May: _____   September: _____

Speaking

Speaking strategy
Ask questions to find out more.

6 Work with a friend. How often does it rain or snow in your country?

How often does it snow in winter?

It often snows in January and February.

7   Watch Part 3 of the story video. Is it hot or cold on Cranky's planet?

145

Writing

1 **Look at Sandy's poster and answer.**

1 What's Sandy's favorite season?
2 What does he do?
3 What does he eat?
4 Where does he live?
5 What's the weather like?

2 **Read Sandy's description and check your answers.**

I LOVE SUMMER!

My favorite season is summer. I like the summer because I go to the beach and I play outside with my friends. I eat watermelon and drink lots of cold water! It sometimes rains in the summer. It's usually hot and sunny. I wear shorts, T-shirts, and sandals. I live in Greece. Greece is in the Northern Hemisphere and summer is in June, July, and August. We don't have school in July or August.

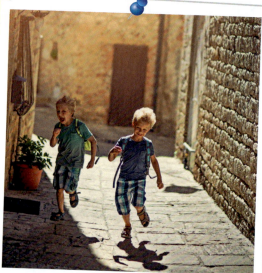

3 **Read the description again. Circle *it* or *it's*.**

4 **Find or draw a picture of your favorite season.** Then go to the Workbook to do the writing activity.

Writing strategy

We can use **It** or **It's** to talk about the weather.
It sometimes gets cold and windy.
It's usually hot and sunny.

Now I Know

1 How are the seasons different? Think about spring and winter. Circle spring words in blue and winter words in green.

> boots   coats   hats   hot soup   ice cream   it's cold
> it's hot   it rains   it snows   it's sunny   it's windy
> playing indoors   playing outside   sandals   skiing
> strawberries   swimming   T-shirts

2 Choose a project.

Make a weather graph.

1. Write at the bottom: *sunny, rainy, snowy, cloudy, windy.*
2. Write on the side the days of the week (Monday to Sunday).
3. Every day, check (✓) the correct weather.
4. Present your graph to the class.

or

Make a coloring game.

1. Choose a season. Draw a picture of a tree with a black pen.
2. Write about the picture: *It's fall. The leaves on the trees are red.*
3. Ask a friend to read and color the picture.
4. Show your picture to the class.

★ ★ ★ **Read and color the stars** ★ ★ ★

 I can understand basic information about times of the year.

 I can describe what the weather is like in my country.

 I can follow the sequence of events in a short text about the seasons.

 I can write about the weather.

147

How are we all different?

Listening
- I can understand simple comparisons between people.

Reading
- I can understand the main points in a short, simple text about people.

Speaking
- I can describe what a person looks like.

Writing
- I can write short, descriptive texts about people I know.

1 Write people you know.

Family	Friends
my mom	

Neighbors	Other
	my teacher

2 Look at the picture and discuss.

1 Where are they?
2 Are they friends, family, or neighbors?
3 What do they like to do together?
4 Do you like doing things with your family?

3 Watch the video and answer.

1 Who's at the top of the family tree?
2 Who's next to Miranda?
3 Who's the oldest in the family?
4 Who's the youngest in the family?

Vocabulary 1

1 **Listen and repeat.**

2 **Listen and number.**

3 **Listen and say.**

4 Read and write the word. Do you know someone who speaks like this? Write their names.

1 "Oh, hi, it's nice to see you! What a beautiful coat you're wearing!" — kind — my grandma.

2 "So, she says to me, "Oh, that's funny," and I say to her, "Yes," then she says, "Would you like a cup of tea?" And I say, … "

3 "I don't like this weather. I don't like this TV program. I don't like this food."

4 "Can I help you with your shopping? I'll carry your bags!"

5 "I work in a grocery store all day. Then, I clean the house, and cook dinner in the evening."

6 "I have a good idea for a story! And I'm painting a picture of the ocean!"

150

5 Think about people you know. Write words to describe them.

My grandpa

My P.E. teacher

My neighbor

My best friend

Pre-reading 1

Reading strategy

Read aloud for expression.

1 Look at the sentences from the story. Read them aloud. Is your voice kind or grumpy? Check (✓).

"What? What are you saying?" shouts Mr. Blake. "I can't hear you! Go away!"

kind ☐

grumpy ☐

151

Reading 1

2 Read *Mr. Blake and the Ball*. Check your answer from Activity 1.

Reading strategy

Read aloud for expression.

Mr. Blake and the Ball

Alex is very **active** and he likes playing ball in the yard. Alex kicks his ball. It goes into his neighbor's yard. His neighbor is Mr. Blake. "Oh no," says Alex. "Mr. Blake shouts a lot. He's **grumpy**!"

"Can you ask Mr. Blake for my ball, please?" he asks his sister, Annie.
"I'm painting," says Annie. She's **creative**.
"Mom, Dad, can you ask Mr. Blake for my ball, please?" asks Alex.
Alex's mom and dad are working and can't help Alex. They're **hardworking**.
"Grandma! Can you please help me?"
"I'm talking on the phone, Alex!" says Grandma. She's very **chatty**!

152

Alex thinks, "I'm usually **shy**, but now I'm ... I'm brave!"
He calls over the fence. "Mr. Blake! Please can I have my ball?"
"What? What are you saying?" shouts Mr. Blake. "I can't hear you!"
"I'm sorry, Mr. Blake. Please, can I have my ball?"
"A wall?" asks Mr. Blake. "What wall?"
"No, a ball!" says Alex. "Look! That blue ball!"
"A ball!" says Mr. Blake. He smiles. "Let's play together!"

Alex jumps over the fence. "Wow, thanks, Mr. Blake. You're very **kind**!"
"Speak louder, please," says Mr. Blake. "I can't hear very well. I'm a bit deaf."

"Oh," thinks Alex. "Mr. Blake doesn't shout because he's grumpy. He shouts because he can't hear very well!" Mr. Blake kicks the ball.

3 Read the story again and circle.

1 Alex likes **running** / **playing ball** in the yard.
2 Alex's ball goes into his **grandma's** / **neighbor's** yard.
3 Alex's grandma is **talking** / **working**.
4 He's a bit **creative** / **shy**.
5 Mr. Blake shouts because he's **grumpy** / **a bit deaf**.

4 Do you sometimes feel grumpy? When? Are your family the same or different?

153

Grammar 1

1   Watch Part 1 of the story video. What day is it?

My grandfather is older than me.

2 Read the grammar box and circle.

> **Grammar**
>
> Me: 8
>
> My brother: 12   I'm **younger** / **older** than my brother.
>
> My sister: 3   I'm **younger** / **older** than my sister.

3 Look at Ben and Jack and write **T** (true) or **F** (false).

1 Ben is taller than Jack. ......
2 Ben's hair is longer than Jack's hair. ......
3 Jack is younger than Ben. ......
4 Jack is older than Ben. ......

5 Think about your family. Write the ages.

Me ....
My mom ....
My dad ....
My friend ....

4 Look at Activity 3 again. Then read and complete.

1 Jack is .... than Ben. (short)
2 Jack's hair is .... than Ben's hair. (long)
3 Jack isn't .... than Ben. (old)
4 Ben isn't .... than Jack. (young)
5 Jack isn't .... than Ben. (tall)

Ben

Jack

6 Measure and write. Use *taller* and *shorter*.

Me and my friends	Height
Me	

I'm _____ than _____ .
_____ is _____ than _____ .

Listening and Speaking

Speaking strategy

Disagree politely.

7 Listen and circle.
2-32

This is **Gina** / **Poppy**. She's **10** / **8**.

This is **Gina** / **Poppy**. She's **10** / **8**.

8 Read and complete.

| longer | older | shorter |
| taller | younger |

1 Poppy is _____ than Gina.
2 Poppy is _____ than Gina.
3 Poppy's hair is *shorter* than Gina's hair.
4 Gina is _____ than Poppy.
5 Gina is _____ than Poppy.
6 Gina's hair is _____ than Poppy's hair.

9 Talk with a friend.

I think I'm taller than you.

No, I don't think so. I'm taller than you.

155

Vocabulary 2

1 Listen and repeat.

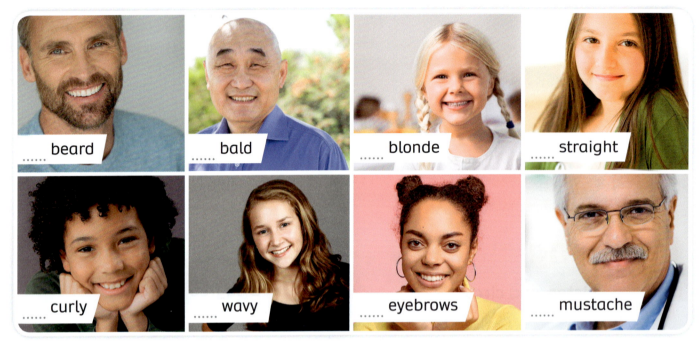

2 Listen and number.

3 Listen and say.

4 Find the differences and write.

A	He has black eyebrows.	He has white eyebrows.
B		
C		
D		

156

5 Look at the picture and write sentences to describe the man.

....
....
....
....
....
....

6 Choose a picture from Activity 1. Then talk about it with a friend.

> She has wavy hair.

> He has big eyebrows.

Pre-reading 2

Reading strategy

Read aloud for expression.

1 Look at the sentences from the text. Read them aloud. Which sentences show someone is speaking? Circle.

Now ask those people about other people in the family. You can ask these questions.

"Grandpa, tell me about your dad. What was he like? Was he **bald**? Do you have a picture?"

157

Reading 2

2 Read *How to Make a Family Album*. Check your answer from Activity 1.

> 📖 **Reading strategy**
>
> Read aloud for expression.

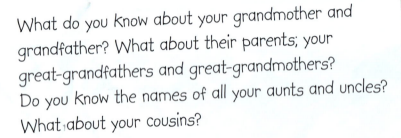
How to Make a Family Album

What do you know about your grandmother and grandfather? What about their parents; your great-grandfathers and great-grandmothers? Do you know the names of all your aunts and uncles? What about your cousins?

To make a family album you can use a photo album or a scrapbook. A scrapbook is good because you can write and draw on the pages, too.

My great-grandmother and great-grandfather

My aunt and uncle

My cousin

First, make a list of all the people you know in your family. Write who they are and their names and surnames.

Dad: James Bright
Grandma: Helen Bright

Now ask those people about other people in the family. You can ask these questions.

"Grandpa, tell me about your dad. What was he like? Was he **bald**? Do you have a picture of him? Can I have a copy of the picture, please?"

"Grandma, what was your mom's name? Was her hair **straight** or **curly**? What were her favorite things?"

Then write those people on your list. Now collect pictures of everyone on your list. Stick the pictures in the album. Don't stick lots of pictures on one page. Stick one or two. Then you can write about the people. Write their names and then write descriptions.

This is a picture of my great-grandmother, Ellen Bright. She was very kind. Her hair was **blonde** and **wavy**.
This is my great-grandfather. His name was Walter Bright. He had brown short, wavy hair. He wasn't bald and didn't have a **mustache**! His **eyebrows** were brown!

Then you can draw or stick pictures of their favorite things next to the pictures.

3 Which pictures show Ellen and Walter Bright? Check (✓).

4 Do you have pictures of your grandparents or great-grandparents? Who do you look like?

159

Grammar 2

1   Watch Part 2 of the story video. Why is Cranky sad?

2 Read the grammar box. Then write the numbers.

> **Grammar**
>
> I'm 8 now. Last year I was 7 .
>
> He's 9 now. Last year he was ....
>
> She's 10 now. Last year she was ....
>
> We're 11 now. Last year we were ....
>
> You're 12 now. Last year you were ....

Cranky's grandfather is orange.
His great-grandfather was orange, too.

3 Read *How to Make a Family Album* again and circle examples of *was* and *were*.

4 Complete the sentences. Choose words from the box.

| short   long   lazy   black   curly |

This year
My hair is short.
His hair is straight.
He's hardworking.
They're tall.
His eyebrows are white.

Last year
My hair ___was long___ .
His hair _____ .
He _____ .
They _____ .
His eyebrows _____ .

160

5 Look and write.

His hair was long, but now it's short.

Speaking

6 Talk about people you know. Use these words.

| cheerful | grumpy | hardworking | lazy |
| long | old | short | shy | tall | young |

My grandfather was cheerful, but now he's grumpy.

7   Watch Part 3 of the story video. Who's older, Cranky, or his brother?

Writing

1 Look at Adam's photo album and answer.

1. Who's creative?
2. Who's hardworking?
3. Who's younger, Adam or his sister?

Hello, I'm Adam.

2 Read Adam's notes and check your answers.

people I like

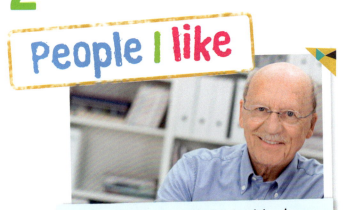

My neighbor is bald but he has a mustache. He's funny and helpful.

My mom and dad are hardworking and kind. My mom is shorter than my dad.

My sister is younger than me. She has wavy, blonde hair. Her birthday was last week. Now she's five! She was happy on her birthday!

My teacher has straight, brown hair. She's very creative.

3 Read the text again. Circle the words about hair.

4 Find or draw pictures of people you know. Then go to the Workbook to do the writing activity.

Writing strategy

We can use two words to describe physical looks. The color word always comes second.
She has *straight*, *brown* hair.
He has *big*, *brown* eyes.

162

Now I Know

1 How are we all different? Sort and write. Add your own ideas.

> He's kind.　　He has a beard.　　She's chatty.　　She has curly hair.

How we look

....

....

....

What we are like

....

....

....

2 Choose a project.

Make a *Guess Who?* card game.

1. Think about a person you know.
2. Write notes about what he or she is like.
3. Write notes about how he or she looks.
4. Talk about the person.
5. Your friends guess the person.

or

Draw a family tree.

1. Draw older people at the top and younger people at the bottom.
2. Draw lines between the people.
3. Write names and stick pictures.
4. Show your family tree to the class.

 **Read and color the stars**

 I can understand simple comparisons between people.

 I can describe what a person looks like.

 I can understand the main points in a short, simple text about people.

 I can write short, descriptive texts about people I know.

11
How do we solve problems?

Listening
- I can understand simple conversations about everyday situations.

Reading
- I can understand the main points in a short, simple text about problem solving.

Speaking
- I can use basic words and phrases to describe objects.

Writing
- I can write a math problem.

164

1 **What can we say when lessons are too difficult? Check (✓).**

"I don't understand." ☐

"I understand this lesson." ☐

"I can't do this." ☐

"Can you help me, please?" ☐

2 **Look at the picture and discuss.**

1 What are they doing?
2 Are they talking?
3 Are they thinking?
4 Do they help each other?

3 11-1 BBC **How many can you see? Watch the video and write.**

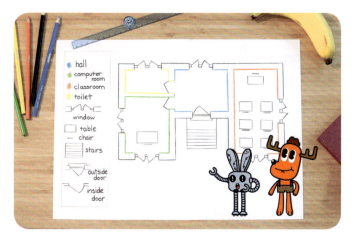

tables ......
windows ......
chairs ......

🇬🇧 British	🇺🇸 American
hall	hallway

165

Vocabulary 1

1 Listen and repeat.

add | subtract | sum | plus
minus | equals | measure | problem

2 Listen and number.

3 Listen and say.

4 Read and write.

Eight plus four equals _12_ .

Five minus four equals _____ .

Add three to four. The answer is _____ .

Subtract five from ten. The answer is _____ .

Measure your English book. How long is it? _____ How wide is it? _____

Solve this problem. Five children have two red and two blue crayons each. How many crayons do they have in total? _____

166

5 What's the teacher saying? Do the sums.

3 + 8 = ...   Three plus eight equals eleven.

10 − 4 = ...

7 + 2 = ...

4 + 3 + 6 = ...

Pre-reading 1

1 Read this problem. Do you know the answer? Check with a friend, then write.

Reading strategy

Check things with friends.

Grace has 15 books. Her brother likes books, too. She gives him three. How many books does Grace have now?

I think the answer is ....

My friend thinks the answer is ....

Reading 1

2 Read *Math Problems!* How many math problems are there?

> 📖 **Reading strategy**
> Check things with friends.

MATH Problems!

When do you do math **problems**? In your math class at school? Yes, but we also use our math skills in other places. We use math at the grocery store, at home, and with our friends. Our math skills can help us find the answers to everyday problems!

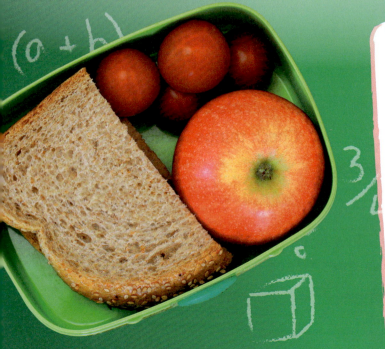

A

Sarah and Joel are going to school. Their mom gives them **two** lunchboxes.

She gives Joel **three** sandwiches and **one** apple. She gives Sarah **four** sandwiches and two apples. How many sandwiches do Sarah and Joel have in total? How many apples?

You **add** three and four.
That **equals** .... sandwiches.
You add two and one.
That equals .... apples.

3 Solve the problems. Then check with a friend.

A 3 + 4 = ... sandwiches, ... apples
B .... candies
C .... toy cars
D .... books
E Which line is longer? ....

168

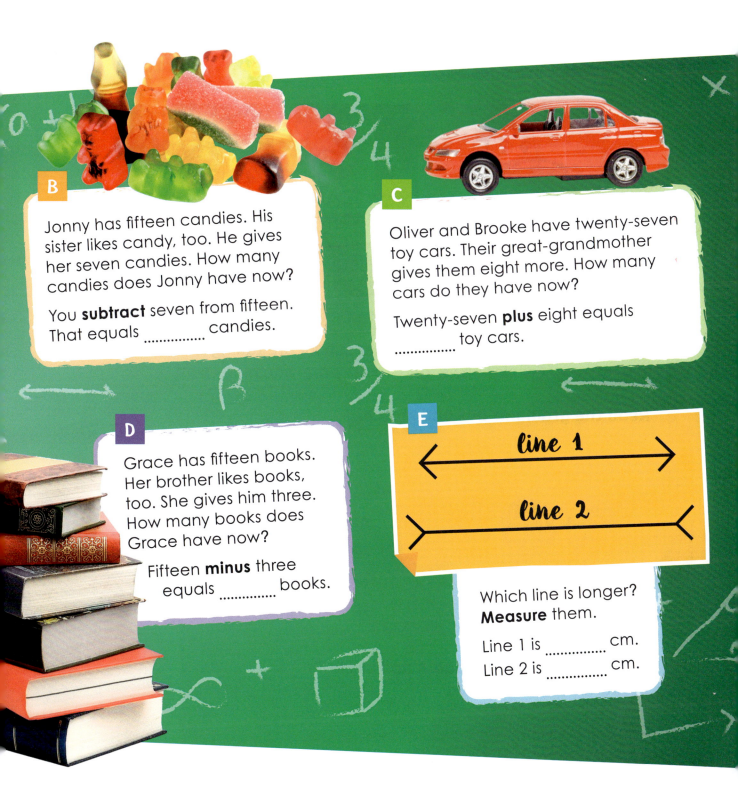

B

Jonny has fifteen candies. His sister likes candy, too. He gives her seven candies. How many candies does Jonny have now?

You **subtract** seven from fifteen. That equals .... candies.

C

Oliver and Brooke have twenty-seven toy cars. Their great-grandmother gives them eight more. How many cars do they have now?

Twenty-seven **plus** eight equals .... toy cars.

D

Grace has fifteen books. Her brother likes books, too. She gives him three. How many books does Grace have now?

Fifteen **minus** three equals .... books.

E

line 1

line 2

Which line is longer? **Measure** them.

Line 1 is .... cm.
Line 2 is .... cm.

4 Look at problem B. How old is Jonny's sister? Add all the numbers in **blue**. Check with a friend.

5 When do you use your math skills? What do you count every day? When do you add or subtract?

169

Grammar 1

1   Watch Part 1 of the story video. How does Suzie help Cranky?

Some children in another school are taking a test. Cranky, Suzie, and Tommy are watching them.

2 Read the grammar box and match.

Grammar

My friends — us

Me and my friends — them

3 Read *Math Problems!* again and circle examples of *us* and *them*.

4 Read and circle.

1 Come and watch me and my dog.
Come and watch **us** / **them** / **me** / **her** play.

2 Can you help my brother and sister?
Can you help **us** / **them** / **me** / **her** with their homework?

3 Mom! I can't do this jigsaw puzzle.
Can you help **us** / **them** / **me** / **her** ?

4 Sara's doctor measures **us** / **them** / **me** / **her** and her little sister.

5 Ask for help. Write *us* or *them*.

1. We don't understand this problem. Can you help _____us_____, please?
2. My friends can't do this sum. Can you help _____?
3. Jade and Tom don't know the answer. Can you tell _____?
4. We don't know the answer. Can you tell _____?
5. How can we make a paper flower? Can you show _____?
6. How can my cousins make a paper flower? Can you show _____?

Listening and Speaking

6 Listen and write T (True) or F (False).
2-41

1. Danny's brother and sister are twins. ......
2. Their birthday is on Sunday. ......
3. They like cars. ......
4. They like robots. ......
5. They like balls. ......
6. They like jigsaw puzzles. ......
7. Danny's friend helps him by asking questions. ......

I like **my car**. I like **it**.
I like **cars**. I like **them**.

7 Play a game with your friend.

- Write things you like and don't like.
- Say the things to your friend.
- Does your friend like the same things?

Pizza!
I like it!
I like it, too!

Big dogs!
I don't like them!
I like them!

171

Vocabulary 2

1 Listen and repeat.

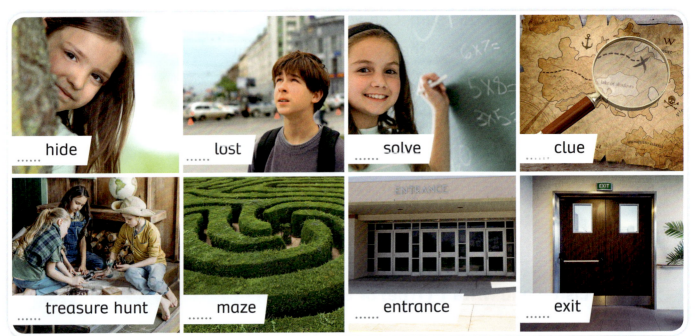

hide | lost | solve | clue
treasure hunt | maze | entrance | exit

2 Listen and number.

3 Listen and say.

4 Write. Then solve the problem. Where's the treasure?

We're having a .... today. The treasure is in a ....

We go in the .... and find a ....

It says, "Where do you go out? That's where the treasure is."

We want to .... the puzzle, but we can't find our friend, Annie.

We say, "Don't .... , Annie!"

We can hear her! She says, "I'm not hiding. I'm .... !"

We walk around the maze. Where's the treasure? Can you help us?

Answer: The treasure is by the ....

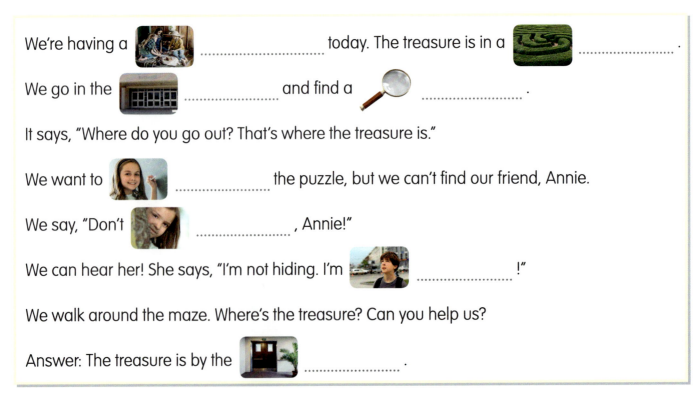

5 Read the clues and find the toys.
Write the toy words on the map.

Clue One:
The doll likes sleeping. She can sleep in this.

Clue Two:
The robot is having a picnic. Quick, find it before it eats all the food!

Clue Three:
The car isn't on the road. It's in the ocean!

Clue Four:
The scooter is going up high. It's lost in the leaves!

Pre-reading 2

1 Look at the problem. Check with a friend.

 Reading strategy

Check things with friends.

What color do you get when you mix blue and yellow together?

The answer is ....

173

Reading 2

2 Read *Escape the Classroom!* What's the treasure you need to find?

> **Reading strategy**
>
> Check things with friends.

Escape the Classroom!

Wow! This is a **treasure hunt**. It isn't in a **maze**. It's in a classroom! The treasure is the key for the classroom door. The key is **lost**! But we can find it! Where is it? Solve the **clues** and open the classroom door.

Find the correct number to open the cupboard. Can you see it?

Clue: How many fingers do you have? How many ears do you have? How many noses do you have? Add the numbers.

The answer is ....

Find the correct animal.

Clue: This animal lives in the Southern Hemisphere, in Australia. It jumps! The babies **hide** in their mother's pouches.

The answer is ....

174

Find the correct letter.

Clue: It's the first letter of this word. There are a lot of these in houses and schools and stores. Sometimes it's an **entrance** and sometimes it's an **exit**.

The answer is _____ .

Find the correct color box.

Clue: The box is the color of the ocean and the color of the sun mixed together.

The answer is _____ .

Find the correct key.

Clue: The key is bigger than the green key and smaller than the yellow key.

The answer is the _____ key!

Congratulations!
You have the key! Now you can escape the classroom!

3 Read the clues and write the answers.

4 Do you sometimes hide? Where's your favorite hiding place?

175

Grammar 2

1   Watch Part 2 of the story video. Where are the schools they're looking at?

We can see them. They can't hear us!

2 Read the grammar box. Write sentences with *them*, *us*, *it*, and *her*.

Grammar

I **can hear** some birds.	I can hear them.
I **can't see** my friend.	
They **can see** my friends and me.	
They **can't hear** the train.	

3 Read *Escape the Classroom!* again and circle an example of *can + find it*.

4 What can you do? Look and complete the sentences with *can* or *can't*.

 lemons   music

I can	see them.	I can't	see it.
I _____	hear them.	I _____	hear it.
I _____	taste them.	I _____	taste it.
I _____	touch them.	I _____	touch it.
I _____	smell them.	I _____	smell it.

176

5 Read the clues and write.

1 They're sometimes white, sometimes gray, and sometimes black. They're in the sky. You can see them, but you can't hear them or touch them. They're _____.

2 It has a lot of doors and windows and rooms. It has desks, chairs, and books. You don't sleep here. You can see it and touch it, but you can't taste it. It's a _____.

3 You often eat this in the summer. It's cold and sweet. It isn't fruit. You can see it, touch it, and taste it. You can't hear it. It's an _____.

Speaking

6 Play the game with a friend.

💬 **Speaking strategy**
Take turns describing something.

- Choose a picture. Don't say what it is.
- Tell your friend about the picture.
- Your friend guesses the picture.

You can taste it. You can smell it. You can touch it. You can't hear it. It's green.

Is it an apple?

Yes, it is.

7   Watch Part 3 of the story video. What does Cranky draw?

Writing

1 **Look at Georgia's picture and predict.**

1 What does she like doing?
2 What does she do first?

2 **Read Georgia's text and check your answers. Then write the answer to the math problem.**

I LOVE Math Problems!

Hi, I'm Georgia. I love math and my hobby is writing math problems. It's easy! First, I think of a sum. For example, ten minus three equals seven. Then I think of people and things. For example, Davy has ten apples. He gives one apple to his sister, one to his mom, and one to his dad. How many apples does Davy have now? The answer is seven! I write the problems and give them to my friends at school.

Here's another problem. Can you solve it?

Cristina has two dolls. Her mom gives her another one. Her dad gives her two. Her grandma gives her three. How many dolls does Cristina have now?

The answer is _____!

3 **Read the text again. Circle *For example*.**

4 **Think of a math problem. Draw pictures for the problem. Then go to the Workbook to do the writing activity.**

Writing strategy

We say **for example** when we want to give extra information. Remember to use a comma.
For example, Davy has ten apples.

178

Now I Know

1 How do we solve problems? What do you do when you have a problem? Check (✓). Then tell a friend.

	always	sometimes	never
I solve it alone.			
I ask my friends for help.			
I ask my parents for help.			
I ask my teacher for help.			

2 Choose a project.

Ask a friend to help you.
1. Think of a problem you have. Make notes.
2. Tell two or three friends about your problem.
3. Listen to their help.
4. Decide who can help you.

or

Draw a treasure map.
1. Hide something in your classroom.
2. Draw a map of your classroom with some clues.
3. Show your map to a friend.
4. Ask your friend to find the treasure!

★ ★ ★ **Read and color the stars** ★ ★ ★

 I can understand simple conversations about everyday situations.

 I can use basic words and phrases to describe objects.

 I can understand the main points in a short, simple text about problem solving.

 I can write a math problem.

12
Why is it good to be outdoors?

Listening
- I can identify events that happened in the past.

Reading
- I can understand short paragraphs about travel.

Speaking
- I can talk about an event in the past.

Writing
- I can write about a place I know.

1 What do you usually see outdoors? Circle.

books	birds	clouds
cows	desks	fish
flowers	horses	pencils
rivers	sheep	the moon
the stars	the sun	trees

2 Look at the picture and discuss.

1 What's the girl doing?
2 Where's this?
3 Does the girl go there often?

3 12-1 BBC Watch the video and answer.

1 What do they take pictures of?
2 Do they use a camera or a tablet?
3 Which picture do you like?

🇬🇧 British	🇺🇸 American
take photos	take pictures

181

Vocabulary 1

1 **Listen and repeat.**

grass | lake | hills | pond
wildlife | meadow | rocks | sand

2 **Listen and number.**

3 **Listen and say.**

4 Plan a day out with friends. Check (✓) the things you like. Then ask a friend and think of a good place to do the things.

	Me	Friend	A good place to do this
fishing			lake
going on boats			
walking on grass			
having picnics			
climbing trees			
watching ducks			
playing with sand			
walking up and running down			
taking pictures of wildlife			

182

5 🗨 Talk with a friend. What do you need for your day out?

What do we need for a day at the beach?

We all need hats for a day at the beach!

Pre-reading 1

1 Look at the sentences from the reading. What are Southern Cassowaries? Check (✓). Circle the words that helped you.

📖 **Reading strategy**

Read on to understand unusual words.

There are some rare animals. Southern Cassowaries live in the forest. They're very big birds.

183

Reading 1

2 Read *Great Outings*. Check your answer from Activity 1.

 Reading strategy
Read on to understand unusual words.

Great Outings

Lake Chapala

Lake Chapala is a big **lake** in Mexico. It's 80 kilometers long and 13 kilometers wide. A lot of birds live on the lake. Pelicans come every winter. Pelicans are big, white birds and they fly from **ponds** and lakes in North America. There are ducks and geese, too.

You can do a lot of things at Lake Chapala. You can go fishing, sail on a boat, ride your bike, or walk in the **hills** and **meadows** close to the lake, or just sit on a big **rock** and take pictures of the **wildlife**.

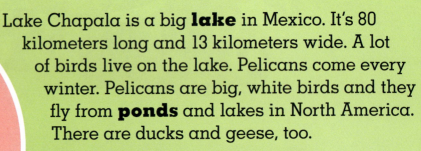

" Last summer my family and I stayed in a hotel by Lake Chapala. I walked by the lake and watched the birds. I have a lot of pictures of the lake. It was a great vacation. "

Daintree forest

Daintree Forest is in North Australia. It's a very big forest. It's enormous! It's full of wildlife. There are thousands of insects, bats, and butterflies in the grass and trees. There are some rare animals. Southern Cassowaries live in the forest. They're very big birds. The tree kangaroo lives in the forest, too.

You can walk up high in Daintree Forest. There's an aerial walkway. That's a road in the sky! It's like a bridge.

> " Last year, I walked on the aerial walkway in Daintree forest. I liked it. It was exciting to see the tree kangaroos! After that we walked up some hills. These were made of **sand**. They're sand dunes. That was completely different! "

3 Read the text again and answer the questions.

1 Where's Lake Chapala?
2 What can you do there?
3 Where's Daintree Forest?
4 What can you see there?

4 Do you like walking? Where do you usually take walks? What do you see and hear?

185

Grammar 1

1 **Watch Part 1 of the story video. Where's the spaceship?**

2 **Look at the grammar box and match.**

The spaceship crashed!
Yes. We watched it!
I didn't like it!

Grammar

Yesterday I ...

watched	to school by bus.
walked	TV.
traveled	up a hill.
talked	to my friends.
looked	tennis.
played	at some old pictures.

I **didn't have** any homework yesterday. I **liked** my day!

3 **Read *Great Outings* again and circle examples of *-ed* words.**

4 **What did you do yesterday? Choose and write.**

> play   cook   collect   watch   wash   do   talk

1. I ………………………………… spaghetti.
2. I ………………………………… to my friends.
3. I ………………………………… video games.
4. I ………………………………… my hands.
5. I ………………………………… stickers.
6. I ………………………………… a movie
7. I ………………………………… my homework

186

5 What did you do yesterday? Write true sentences.

✓	✗
I washed my hands.	I didn't cook spaghetti.

Listening and Speaking

6 🎧 2-50 Listen to Lewis talking about his day yesterday. Check (✓) or cross (✗).

1. He traveled to school by bus. ☐
2. He picked some flowers. ☐
3. He cooked lunch. ☐
4. He played basketball. ☐
5. He washed his dad's car. ☐
6. He watched a movie. ☐

7 💬 Talk about Lewis's day. Then talk about your day yesterday.

> Lewis walked to school. I didn't walk to school.

> Lewis didn't travel to school by bus. I traveled to school by bus.

Vocabulary 2

1 Listen and repeat.

fins · snorkel · water wings · air mattress
hotel · shell · seaweed · sandcastle

2 Listen and number.

3 Listen and say.

4 Read and write the correct word.

1. I can breathe underwater because I'm wearing my ....

2. I'm swimming fast! I have .... on my feet!

3. I'm digging and building an amazing .... !

4. Oh, this is a beautiful .... I collect them!

5. My little brother is wearing .... on his arms.

6. We're playing in the ocean. We're sitting on our ....

7. We're staying in a .... I have a big room!

8. My mom is funny. She has some .... on her head. She says she has green hair now!

188

5 You're going on vacation! Talk with friends. What do you want to take and do? Write.

	City vacation	Beach vacation
Things to take on vacation:	....	....
Things to do on vacation:	....	....

6 Talk with another group about your vacation.

Pre-reading 2

> **Reading strategy**
> Read on to understand unusual words.

1 Look at this sentence from the reading. Circle the words you don't understand.

 Samira's favourite thing was beachcombing with her mum.

2 What's the next sentence? Check (✓).

A beach has sand and rocks. ☐

Beachcombing is looking for seaweed, shells, stones, driftwood and sea glass. ☐

Samira and Teo liked swimming underwater in the ocean. ☐

189

Reading 2

3 Read *Samira's Sea Glass Collection*. Check your answer from Activity 2.

Reading strategy
Read on to understand unusual words.

Samira's Sea Glass Collection

Last year, Samira and her family stayed in a small **hotel** on the beach. The beach was sandy and the sea was turquoise. Samira's little sister Alma liked making **sandcastles**. Her brother Teo didn't like making sandcastles.

Samira and Teo had **snorkels**, masks and **fins**. They snorkelled for hours and saw lots of colourful fish in the sea.

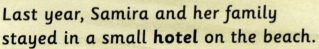

But Samira's favourite thing was beachcombing with her mum. Beachcombing is looking for **seaweed**, **shells**, stones, driftwood and sea glass.

Samira loved collecting the pretty sea glass. Soon, her buckets were full.

190

Samira did so many activities on holiday. One day, Samira and her family wanted to make a sea glass heart on the beach. The heart sparkled on the beach.

Samira loved her collection of sea glass. The only problem was that she didn't know what to do with her collection.

Samira decided to fill a big jar with the sea glass. Back home, it was her memory jar of the sea glass beach.

4 Read the story again and circle.

1. The hotel was **big** / **small**.
2. Teo **loved** / **didn't like** building sandcastles.
3. Mom **went** / **didn't go** snorkeling with the children.
4. Samira filled her memory jar with **shells** / **sea glass**.

5 Do you go to different places during vacation? Where do you go?

Grammar 2

1 **Watch Parts 2 and 3 of the story video. Is it Cranky's birthday?**

Did Cranky like his gift?
Yes, he did!

2 Read the grammar box. Write *did* or *Did*.

> **Grammar**
>
> ……………… you stay in a hotel?
> **No**, I **didn't**.
> ……………… she stay with your grandma?
> **Yes**, she ……………… .

3 Read *Samira's Sea Glass Collection* again and circle *did* and *didn't*.

4 Read and match.

1 Did you go on vacation?
2 Did you stay in a hotel?
3 Did your brother play on an air mattress?
4 Did your sister jump in the ocean?
5 Did you meet new friends?
6 Did your dad watch wildlife?
7 Did your mom pick some flowers?
8 Did you enjoy your vacation?

a Yes, he did. It was very funny!
b Yes, I did. I want to go there again.
c No, she didn't. She doesn't like the ocean.
d Yes, he did. He watched birds.
e No, I didn't. I stayed in a house.
f Yes, I did. I always go on vacation in the summer.
g No, I didn't. I'm shy!
h Yes, she did. They were beautiful!.

12

5 Read and match.

travel — by plane
play — beach volleyball
visit — your grandparents
cook — on a barbecue
walk — up a hill
watch — birds in the sky

6 Write questions about last summer.
Then ask a friend and write the answers.

Did you travel by plane?

....
....
....
....
....

Speaking

7 What did you do yesterday?
Play a guessing game.

Speaking strategy
Take turns speaking.

I cooked something on a barbecue.   I walked somewhere.
I collected something.   I visited someone.

I cooked something on a barbecue yesterday!

Did you cook chicken?

Did you cook fish?

No, I didn't.

Yes, I did!

193

Writing

1 Look at Charlie's picture and answer.

1 Where's his favorite place?
2 What wildlife can you see there?
3 Why does Charlie like being outdoors?

2 Read Charlie's vacation report and check your answers.

THE ROCKIES

HOME | ABOUT | DESTINATION | BLOG | PICTURES

I love being outdoors! My favorite place is the mountains. Last winter we traveled to Canada and stayed in a hotel in the Rocky Mountains. I fished in the lakes, skied in the snow, and walked in the forest. There's a lot of wildlife in the Rockies.

I have a good camera on my tablet. It's like a real one. I have a picture of a Bighorn Ram. Bighorn Rams are like very big sheep. I like being outdoors because you get a lot of fresh air and you can do so many different things. I'm never bored outdoors!

3 Read the text again. Circle *is like* and *are like*.

4 Find or draw a picture of your favorite outdoor place. Then go to the Workbook to do the writing activity.

Writing strategy

We use **is like** and **are like** to say how things are similar.
Bighorn Rams **are like** *very big sheep.*

194

Now I Know

1 Why is it good to be outdoors? Sort the places.

hill	lake	living room
park	playground	
meadow	yard	school

Outdoors	Indoors

2 What things do you do outdoors? Talk with a friend.

3 Choose a project.

Present your favorite place.
1. Think of your favorite outdoor place.
2. Find or draw pictures.
3. Make notes on what you can do and why you like it.
4. Present it to the class.

or

Make a vacation postcard.
1. Stick or draw a picture of a vacation place on one side of a card.
2. On the other side, write where you are.
3. Write what you did yesterday.
4. Show your card to the class.

★ ★ ★ **Read and color the stars** ★ ★ ★

 I can identify events that happened in the past.

 I can talk about an event in the past.

 I can understand short paragraphs about travel.

 I can write about a place I know.

195

Wordlist

Unit 1

Key vocabulary

art
bored
busy
computer science
difficult
easy
important
interesting
math
music
P.E.
piano practice
science
tired
violin practice
worried

Readings

chalk
count
draw
kick
learn new things
play the drums
polite
punch
roll
shout
slip
stretch
take turns

Unit 2

Key vocabulary

angry
bamboo
camel
cheetah
crocodile

dangerous
desert
fat
forest
funny
jungle
kangaroo
lazy
mountain
ocean
panda
river
savannah
seal
smart
snake
strong
thin
whale

Readings

Africa
Atlantic Ocean
chase
China
hard
hump
insect
plane
Sahara Desert
smell
South America
strange
vitamin
world

Unit 3

Key vocabulary

cap
flip flops
foggy
hail

lightning
robe
scarf
sleet
slippers
sneakers
storm
sunglasses
sweat suit
thunder
tornado
windy

Readings

air
amazing
blow
boots
change
cloud
coat
fall
go around
grass
puddle
sky
snow
splash
sun
tree
water
wet

Unit 4

Key vocabulary

bank
bookstore
computer store
factory
fields
gas station
library
market
movie theater
playground
restaurant

small town
street
toy store
traffic
train station

Readings

across from
behind
city
closed
in front of
librarian
machine
money
neighborhood
open
out of order
shout
town

Unit 5

Key vocabulary

adventure playground
aquarium
arts center
balloon
bowling alley
burger
candle
card
cupcake
fruit salad
ice rink
milkshake
nature center
popcorn
swimming pool
theme park

Readings

candies
decorate
decorations
frosting

invitation
preparing
pretend
putting up decorations

Unit 6

Key vocabulary

astronaut
check
chef
clean
cook
dentist
doctor
fix
hairdresser
help
perform
photographer
police officer
study
vet
whistle

Readings

counts
dog walker
equipment
float
gravity
guitar
mistake
neighbor
packages
problem
Space Station
spaceship
walks

Unit 7

Key vocabulary

badminton
baseball
bounce
catch

field hockey
hit
hold
horseback riding
kick
paddleboarding
ping-pong
pull
push
skiing
throw
water polo

Readings

board
helmet
life jacket
medal
swimming cap
team
whistle

Unit 8

Key vocabulary

braces
breathe
chew
dirty
feel
hear
hurt
mouthwash
relax
rinse
smell
taste
toothache
toothbrush
toothpaste
touch

Readings

bite
blanket
chew
cut

dark
fall out
footsteps
friendly
grow
hide
noise
sharp
straight
tear

Unit 9

Key vocabulary

January
February
March
April
May
June
July
August
September
October
November
December
spring
summer
fall
winter
seasons
world
North
South

Readings

cloudy
equator
fat
forest
half
hungry
insects
leaves
maps
Northern Hemisphere
raining

shining
Southern Hemisphere
tail
thin

Unit 10

Key vocabulary

active
bald
beard
blonde
chatty
creative
curly
eyebrows
grumpy
hardworking
helpful
kind
mustache
shy
straight
wavy

Readings

active
album
brave
copy
deaf
fence
great-grandfather
great-grandmother
scrapbook
shouts
smiles

Unit 11

Key vocabulary

add
clue
entrance
equals
exit
hide

lost
maze
measure
minus
plus
problem
solve
subtract
sum
treasure hunt

forest
jar
pelicans
rare
sea glass
sparkled
turquoise
wide

Readings

escape
everyday
key
mix
pouch
skills
total

Unit 12

Key vocabulary

air mattress
fins
grass
hill
hotel
lake
meadow
pond
rocks
sand
sandcastle
seaweed
shell
snorkel
water wings
wildlife

Readings

aerial walkway
beachcombing
bridge
bucket
driftwood
enormous